STAND UP!

BE AN UPSTANDER AND MAKE A DIFFERENCE

BY

WENDY L. MOSS, PHD

Magination Press • Washington, DC
American Psychological Association

This book is dedicated to all of the peer mentors (also known as peer ambassadors and peer leaders) with whom I have worked. You have modeled how to be kind and altruistic and have shown the courage to work to make the world a better and more peaceful place! Thank you!—WM

Books for Kids From the
American Psychological Association

Book design by Melissa Jane Barrett
Printed by Lake Book Manufacturing, Inc., Melrose Park, IL

Library of Congress Cataloging-in-Publication Data
Names: Moss, Wendy (Wendy L.), author.
Title: Stand up! : be an upstander and make a difference / by Wendy Moss.
Description: Washington, DC : Magination Press, [2019]
Identifiers: LCCN 2018050524 | ISBN 9781433829635 (hardcover) |
ISBN 1433829630 (hardcover)
Subjects: LCSH: Caring in children—Juvenile literature. | Kindness—Juvenile literature. | Courage in children—Juvenile literature. | Assertiveness in children—Juvenile literature. | Social justice—Juvenile literature.
Classification: LCC BF723.C25 M67 2019 | DDC 177/.7—dc23 LC record available at https://lccn.loc.gov/2018050524

Manufactured in the United States of America
10 9 8 7 6 5 4 3 2 1

CONTENTS

INTRODUCTION

DO YOU WANT TO MAKE THE WORLD A BETTER PLACE?
Maybe you want to change how kids at school or family members treat each other. Maybe you want to change how groups of people are treated or you want to stop animal cruelty or end world hunger. Maybe you want to change how you treat other people when you are upset. After all, you are a human being and human beings make mistakes.

It really does take just one person to start to make changes in the world. Do you want to be that person? If so, keep reading.

You may doubt that one child or teenager could really make a difference when adults have often sought world peace without success. Clearly, you can't fly like Wonder Woman or scale walls like Spiderman, but you could be a hero to some people by speaking up and making small differences that may then lead to bigger and bigger differences.

In this book, you will learn ways to become an Upstander—that means a person who stands up to support fairness and respect while also trying to decrease bullying and injustice. If you believe in yourself, are willing to learn new skills, and set reachable goals, you're on your way!

You will soon read about kids who have stayed motivated, even when people around them didn't always believe in them or when their goals seemed unattainable at first. While the examples in the book are composites drawn from what I have learned from talking

to many, many kids over the years, the experiences and thoughts shared here are common among many kids like you who want to make a difference in their community and the world. Hopefully you will find some ideas and strategies that work for you. You will also get the chance to read about some actual people in history, such as Martin Luther King, Jr., who made a difference by standing up for equality and fair treatment.

This book will take you through ways to be an Upstander, including being kind to yourself, having empathy for others, knowing that positive and negative actions can be powerful and affect others, and understanding how to deal with conflicts. You will learn how to tell the difference between reachable goals and goals that might be too much to deal with right now. Upstanders know how to think about a rule and decide whether it is fair or unfair, the possible ways to address problems, and how to work with others toward common goals. There are lots of actions you can take to share positivity and model respect for others, and you will get a chance to focus on some of these skills as you read through this book.

You already made the first big step toward making a difference in the world by caring enough to open this book. Thank you for your efforts to be compassionate toward others and wanting to reach goals that can lead to positive change!

1

BEING AN UPSTANDER

CAN YOU IMAGINE HOW WONDERFUL THINGS WOULD BE if we all got along, respected each other, had no bullying or wars, and looked out for one another? While this may seem like a huge goal, each of us has the power to make things better . . . or worse. Do you want to make things better for yourself, people you know, and others in the world? You don't have to be an adult to make the world a better place.

Let's focus on what you do every day to help yourself and others. Have you already stood up to voice your support for fair treatment of kids and adults? Would you like to learn how to do this more often or more effectively? Maybe you haven't reached out to support others yet, but you want to know how to do that. This book can help!

As a kid, you see lots of social situations: in school, at friends' homes, at sporting events and activities, and so on. You may see more than the adults, because some children and teens tease or upset others when grown-ups aren't watching. Sometimes kids might not go to adults for help, but you know that they feel sad, confused, or anxious. Or, you may even find yourself in situations where you feel that some rules aren't fair for all people and you want to change them. If you see these situations, how do you handle them? In other words, what kind of bystander are you?

Try taking this brief questionnaire to figure it out. For each situation, decide which of the three reactions is closest to how you would respond. This isn't a test. You can't fail it. Hopefully it will help you start to think about how you handle situations around you.

Quiz

1. At recess, you see a few girls teasing another girl in your grade about how she has no friends and never will because she's "so weird." Do you:
   a. turn your back and walk away because you don't want the girl to think you agree with those who are doing the teasing?
   b. smile when you hear the teasing because you are nervous or don't want the girls to start picking on you too?
   c. try to find a way to help the girl, even if you're not sure how to do this yet?

2. You see a YouTube video or a commercial about a social issue, like animals being mistreated, homelessness, or kids who have serious medical issues. Do you:
   a. change what you are watching because you don't want to feel sad?
   b. make fun of the issues with your friends?
   c. think that, one day, you might want to help those in need?

3. Every day while riding the bus to school, you see a younger boy who sits alone and no one ever tries to talk with him. Do you:
   a. assume he's okay and hang out with your friends?
   b. talk about the boy with your friends and try to imagine what's wrong with him?
   c. think about what you could do to see if he's okay sitting alone?

4. If you hear that one of your friends is being teased because he doesn't have a father in his life, do you:
   a. ignore the teasing and wait to hang out with that friend after school, so no one knows that you are friends?
   b. smile when kids make jokes about the issue, but not in front of your friend?
   c. tell the other kids that it's not funny or kind to ever tease anyone, and that this is a particularly emotional situation?

5. A girl in your grade has speech problems and often mispronounces words. She is also a little shy. At recess, you hear two popular kids mimicking her and laughing. When the girl walks by, you notice that she overhears the teasing, starts to cry, but keeps walking. Do you:
   a. distance yourself from the kids who are making the jokes, because you know what they are doing is wrong?
   b. smile when the others mimic her, because you think she's probably used to the teasing and should work harder to speak more clearly?
   c. approach the girl who has speech problems and let her know that not everyone is ridiculing her?

If you answered mostly 'a', then you are likely being a bystander who might not make a situation more difficult for someone but does not try to stop a negative situation.
If you answered mostly 'b', then you are likely being a bystander who might contribute to a negative situation, either accidentally or on purpose.
If you answered mostly 'c', then you are likely being an Upstander who tries to stop a negative situation.

Three Kinds of Bystanders

The good news is that you can always change the kind of bystander you are if you are not happy with how you act when you see an injustice or situation where someone is upset. A bystander is not someone who starts a problem. A bystander simply is there, watching situations where others may feel supported, cared about, isolated, rejected, or ridiculed, for example.

Many people talk about bystanders only regarding bullying situations. In this book, you will get a chance to think about how you could react in many situations, not all of which are negative. For instance, if a friend wins the spelling bee, do you congratulate him and offer to help him practice for the next competition? Do you ignore the accomplishment? Do you ignore your friend entirely because you are jealous? See? Even in this positive situation, you have a choice of how you respond to the world around you.

Throughout this book, all three types of bystanders will discover how to intervene when problems arise, overcome their possible fears of standing up for others, manage self-doubts about speaking up, and figure out when to get assistance.

Neutral

There are bystanders who don't make a situation worse, but don't really do anything to improve it either. Their behavior is neutral. In the questionnaire, the responses listed next to the letter 'a' describe this type of behavior.

Bystanders might behave neutrally because they:

- are shy (they don't feel comfortable speaking up or taking a leadership role);
- believe others would handle the situation better;
- don't know how to handle the situation;
- don't notice the situation or problem;

- are fearful about becoming a target and being bullied
  if they try to help a person who is currently the target
  (a target is a person getting picked on, similar to the
  term victim but a victim has no options and often a
  target has some choices, especially with your help!).

Some people may not care about an injustice or prefer to focus on fun times and friends. However, assuming all bystanders who act neutrally don't care is really pre-judging them. They may want to help but may not know how.

Negative

Some bystanders behave in a way that contribute to a negative situation. If you selected several 'b' responses in the questionnaire, this may describe your behavior, but this does not mean you are a bully. This does not even mean you want to ever make another person feel uncomfortable.

You may wonder why you, or anyone, would want to make a negative situation worse. But these bystanders don't always mean to hurt others, even if they seem entertained when someone is being mistreated. Sometimes, bystanders may even know that one person plans to upset or even bully another and decide to keep it a secret because it makes them feel special to have this information or because they are riddled with anxiety and not sure what else to do.

Bystanders may behave in a way that contributes to a negative situation because they:

- want the person who is mistreating others to like them so they don't get mistreated too;
- don't know what else to do;
- are nervous and laughing because they are uneasy, not because they are entertained;
- feel that they need to be loyal to friends, even when they are mistreating others;

DOUGLAS'S STORY

Douglas had a reputation in his grade for being mean and for liking when other kids got teased.

In fact, though, Douglas never really teased anyone.

So, why would anyone think Douglas was mean?

Douglas was good friends with a kid named Jacob. When Douglas talked to his parents about Jacob, he told them he was a really nice and smart guy, and that they had fun together.

What he didn't tell his parents was that Jacob often picked on two other boys in their grade. He called them names and even pushed them against the walls between classes.

While Douglas didn't like this side of Jacob, he wanted to be a true friend and stood by him no matter what.

When Jacob was acting cruelly, Douglas just smiled and even sometimes laughed until he was relieved that the mistreatment was over.

- Do you think that Douglas was a bully?

- Could Douglas have handled the situation differently?

- What would you have done?

- Do you think being a true friend means accepting all of your friend's actions?

- fear having no friends if they don't hang out with the person who is making hurtful choices;

If you don't want to be this type of bystander, here are a few questions to ask yourself:
- What would happen if I walked away whenever my friend started to tease someone?
- If my friend might tease me for not laughing at his hurtful comments to others, is he really my friend?
- Do I have true friends, who respect my feelings and whom I am proud to be with?
- If my friend is bullying someone, could I distract her by starting another activity or by telling an adult?
- Do I like how others view me when I'm laughing with the person who is teasing or excluding others?

Positive

The goal of this book is to help readers become positive bystanders, also known as Upstanders. Upstanders stand up for themselves and others. They are caring people who want to help others and are willing to help others. A person is considered to be an Upstander when he or she prevents, or tries to prevent, someone from being bullied—but Upstanders act in less extreme situations as well! In the questionnaire at the start of this chapter, an Upstander would mostly answer 'c' to the questions.

Upstanders try to be positive role-models who make a difference in the world around them. After reading this book, you will gain ideas about how to handle situations that you feel need to be changed. You can also learn some important skills to help you along the way, like perspective taking, conflict resolution, and collaboration.

Upstanders generally:
- care about others;
- want a more peaceful and positive world;

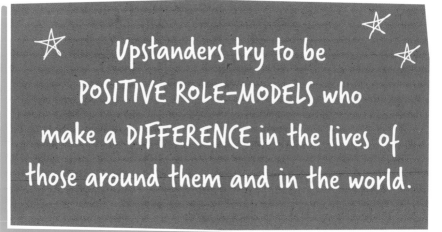

Upstanders try to be POSITIVE ROLE-MODELS who make a DIFFERENCE in the lives of those around them and in the world.

- have basic ideas of how to stand up for themselves and others;
- have some confidence in themselves;
- have a support group of friends and adults who they can talk to about their own feelings and concerns.

The confusing part is that bystanders who behave neutrally or even negatively may share in these Upstander characteristics, and an Upstander may face the same challenges as the other two types of bystanders. Here's the difference: even at the risk of not being totally successful or not having everyone applauding their efforts, Upstanders stand up for others. They are focused on righting the wrongs in the world and are willing to face anxiety and self-doubt.

Are you an Upstander? Are you a positive role-model who cares about the needs of those around you? You might not even need to confront a bully, but you would need to be aware of when another person could use your help. You will also need to be open to helping another person if he asks for help and you feel it's safe and appropriate to support him.

ABBY'S STORY

Abby worked hard to be an Upstander and help others out. She wanted to stand up for kids who were being bullied, but doing so still made her a little nervous. She was an Upstander, though, because she cared about supporting others and being a role-model. Olivia, age 11, was a classmate of Abby's. Olivia was quiet and had only one close friend, but they weren't together in the same social studies class. Prior to a big test, Olivia realized that her social studies notes weren't complete since she had been out ill for a week. Olivia looked around at her classmates and decided to ask Abby for help. She picked Abby because Abby always seemed to respect and accept others. Abby was nice and funny and Olivia hoped to develop a friendship with her.

When Abby learned that Olivia needed help, she could have said, "Sorry, I have to run" or "I took the notes, so they're mine." In other words, "I don't want to focus on your needs." Instead, Abby looked over the pages in Olivia's notebook, found the gap in her notes, and promised to make a copy of her own notes for Olivia by the end of the day.

Olivia feared that Abby would forget or not care to show up at their designated meeting place right after school ended. Sure enough, though, Abby showed up and gave Olivia a copy of her notes. One of Abby's friends saw the exchange and later said, "I can't believe you and Olivia talked. She barely ever talks." Abby smiled and said, "I'm glad she trusted me enough to ask for help."

- Do you think that Abby acted like an Upstander?
- What would you have done?

Would you like others to know that they can count on you? Since you are reading this book, the answer is probably yes! This book can help you learn ways to build a reputation as a positive bystander, or Upstander. Imagine calling a kid who has been out sick, even though you aren't best friends, just to let her know that you hope she feels better soon. That could have a positive impact on her, but also on anyone else who learns of your action.

What an Upstander Can Do

- If you see a classmate being picked on, ask her to join your group. It's a lot harder to bully someone who is in a group.
- If there is an isolated kid in your school, compliment him on something specific. Don't just make something up, though. A thoughtful compliment from another student could really make him feel special and appreciated. Your words might end up being the highlight of his day.
- Be a role-model in how you treat others and yourself. If you are a respectful, honest Upstander in class, at recess, at sporting events, and on the bus, others will notice.

> ☆ A thoughtful compliment from ☆ another student could really make him feel special. Your words might end up being the highlight of his day. ☆

- Be an Upstander at home too. For example, referee between your siblings when they are arguing. Show them how to respectfully work out a disagreement.
- Take on an issue that means something to you (e.g., discrimination; teasing; bullying; certain school rules). How you do this is important. You'll read a lot about how to do this in as you explore later chapters.
- Notice if another person needs help, then offer to help, if appropriate. If you offer to carry a few books for your teacher, help a new student find his classroom, or volunteer to do an extra chore at home, you can show that you value altruism. That means that you value doing things just because they are the right things to do and because you care about others.

Stand Up to Bullying

If you see a person who is purposely bothering or even bullying others, you might want to yell or publicly embarrass her so she will start acting more caring and compassionate. There is nothing wrong with feeling anger, frustration, or even outrage. How you express your emotions, though, is important. You don't want to bully the person who is bullying others, even if your motivation is that you care about someone and want to end mistreatment.

Think about some of the famous activists, Nobel Laureates, and their messages that were heard despite their respectful demeanor. Martin Luther King, Jr. (activist for civil rights), Malala Yousafzai (teenage activist who supported the rights of girls to attend school and youngest Nobel Laureate), and Elie Wiesel (Holocaust survivor who spoke up for human rights) are just a few famous role models who showed that individuals can be heard while acting as respectful Upstanders and without resorting to violence.

The following are some ideas for how to be an Upstander when you see bullying or mistreatment.

When the Aggressor is Your Friend

If you see the kind and funny side to your friend but don't like how he treats others, should you end the friendship? Not necessarily. What can you do? What would you do?

Let's review two tips that you might find helpful:

- If your friend is doing the teasing, you could let him know that you aren't entertained or enjoying it. You could say: "Hey, this isn't fun. Let's do something else," or "Ease up on teasing him. He's actually okay when you get to know him."
- Avoid publically confronting your friend, though, so that he's not focused on his possible feelings of embarrassment or even betrayal and can really listen to what you are saying. Find the right time to let him know how it makes you feel when he bullies or upsets other kids. You'll learn about how to use 'I' messages in Chapter 5, which could help you in these situations.

Being an Upstander and sticking to your values isn't always easy. When you like someone who isn't acting like an Upstander, you don't have to become her teacher. However, you also don't have to simply accept her actions or words.

Try These Quick Comments

If you see mistreatment, here are some quick comments that you might consider saying:

- "We like her!" This lets the target know that she is not alone, while letting the person who is acting aggressively (verbally or physically) know that others will stand with this target and support her;
- "Not funny!" This is best said if the person teasing is your friend; just remember to say it privately so as not to embarrass him;
- "Let's get on with the game." Distract the aggressor until you can figure out how else to respond.

Tell Someone

If speaking up to the aggressor might put you in danger, or if the target seems to be in danger, it's definitely time to tell an adult. This is not tattling; it's just telling. Tattling is generally when you tell on someone because you want that person to get in trouble. Telling is when you want to improve a situation. Chapter 5 will help you figure out when to report issues. For now, just keep in mind that it's okay to sometimes tell others, especially adults, who might be able to help.

Upstanders Are Perfect . . . Not!

Upstanders are human, and human beings aren't perfect. If you want to be an Upstander, but are worried that you can't because you had a fight with your brother last week, that just means you know it's hard to always be a role-model, especially when you are upset.

Upstanders work on controlling their temper and calmly dealing with frustration. In the next chapter, you can learn how to do this. For now, though, pay attention to when you lose your cool and when you are proud of your choices. Having this information can help you understand yourself better, so you can act as an Upstander more often. It's great that you care and are motivated to be an Upstander! Compliment yourself for that.

> ### ▶ START SMALL! ◀
>
> Smile or say "Hi!" to three kids who you don't normally talk to each day. It's one way to let them know that you acknowledge them and care.
>
> If you try this, think about how it made you feel the first time. Think about how it made you feel after you did it for a while. Are you getting more comfortable connecting with others in this way? Hopefully, you can be a role-model to show other students that they can also connect with new people, starting with a simple "Hi."

2

BEING KIND TO YOURSELF

THE PERSON YOU KNOW BEST IS THE PERSON YOU ARE with twenty-four hours each day, seven days a week—YOU! Knowing how to identify your own feelings, be supportive of yourself, cope with frustration, and be self-confident will be useful when you later try to help others.

Luckily, you don't need all of these skills all the time to be an Upstander. Recognizing the differences in how you feel during a tough day and a positive day can help you to understand the range of emotions that others might have too. Once you are aware of all these feelings, you may be better able to identify when someone else needs support.

If you truly understand how to be a friend to yourself, others may notice; you can then be a role model by accepting yourself, even though like most people, you aren't perfect. You can also use this accepting attitude to be a role-model in how you treat others.

Being kind to yourself is not always as easy as it might sound. Even if you think you are ready to support both yourself and those around you, you can still learn something in this chapter. If you spend time really focusing on the skills in this chapter, then you can use this knowledge to help others.

The questionnaire below will help you think about whether you need to work on some skills that would allow you to be kind to yourself or if you already have a good handle on how to do this. For each situation, decide which of the three reactions is closest to how you would respond. Remember: this isn't a test. Hopefully, it will help you recognize how you feel about yourself and how you cope with your emotions.

Quiz

1. You suddenly have lots of things to do. They are all important and have approaching deadlines. Do you:
   a. lose sleep and act irritably toward others, blaming your stress on how others are pressuring you rather than focusing on dealing with the expectations?
   b. know that you are feeling overwhelmed, but hide it because you aren't sure what to do about it?
   c. know that you are feeling overwhelmed, use learned skills to calm yourself, and then strategize to get through everything you need to do?

2. When you don't meet the high expectations you have for yourself—like when you don't get picked to be on the travel soccer team or you get a grade that disappoints you—do you:
   a. get mad at yourself and feel like you are less capable?
   b. remain calm but lower your expectations for the future?
   c. calmly try to figure out what you could do differently to reach your goals in the future?

3. If you try a sport or activity for the first time and struggle to do it, do you:
   a. use negative self-talk, such as "I'm such an idiot," because you are frustrated with yourself?
   b. question whether you could do better and hesitate to try it again?
   c. use positive self-talk, such as "I had the courage to try! I knew I wouldn't be perfect, but it was fun and I want to keep working at it"?

4. Do you know when you are feeling anxious, angry, sad, nervous, or when you have other feelings?
   a. No. I try not to focus on my feelings since I don't think it's worth it.
   b. Yes. I know how I feel, but I'm not sure how that might be helpful to me.
   c. Yes. I know how I feel, and I know that my feelings are giving me important information about myself (e.g., "I'm nervous right now, so I am going to try to calm down before the test.").

5. How I feel about myself:
   a. changes every day, depending on if I do something well or not.
   b. is usually positive, but if someone gets angry with me, I feel like a loser.
   c. is consistently good. If someone gets angry with me or I don't do something well, I try to deal with the issue rather than focus on whether I'm feeling good about being me.

If you answered mostly 'a', then you are likely in the process of learning about yourself, how to feel good about yourself, and how to deal with the stresses you experience.

If you answered mostly 'b', then you are likely on the road to being reflective and confident, but could benefit from some tips.

If you answered mostly 'c', then you have self-awareness and know that it's okay to not succeed after your first attempt at something new. You are willing to take some healthy risks, and you may even know how to deal with strong feelings.

Being an Upstander Starts With Understanding Yourself

If you want to understand how others feel (so you know when to step in and help), it's important to understand your own feelings first. Also, knowing how to be kind and accepting of yourself and having self-confidence are important because they can affect your behavior, choices, willingness to speak up, and even how comfortable you are reaching out to help others. In this chapter, you will learn how to identify your own feelings, help yourself to feel better (so that you can eventually help others to do the same thing), deal with frustration (so you are able to handle situations instead of being overwhelmed with feelings), and build up your confidence. Learning these skills can often make it a bit easier for you to then start to make a difference in your world.

Know How You Feel

Do you know how you feel most of the time? Some people know a lot about their feelings, but others don't focus on feelings unless they are experiencing very strong emotions at a particular time. When a person takes on a challenge and masters it, she might experience feelings of happiness and pride. Or she might feel nervous because she feels pressure to then take on an even harder challenge. If a person is moving to another country, he might have mixed feelings, due to the sadness of leaving friends and the anxiety and excitement about the new adventure of going to a new place. Understanding how you feel lets you learn more about yourself!

There is rarely, if ever, a time when all people have the exact same emotion in the same situation. This isn't odd at all; we are all different. You are the expert on the feelings that you have in particular situations. Feelings teach us when we need support, when we want to repeat an experience that previously led to happiness, or when we need to use coping strategies to decrease anxiety, sadness, frustration, or anger.

SEAN'S STORY

When people don't focus on how they feel, their feelings sometimes show up in surprising ways. For example, Sean, age 13, was an athlete and an honor roll student. His friends described him as always being calm and cool. Sean felt that this was an accurate description. However, at home one night, he was annoyed by everything. He insulted his father's cooking and he tossed his brother's football out the window after he found it on his side of their shared room. Later that evening, he started yelling at his parents because he could hear them talking down the hall when he was trying to study. Eventually, his yelling turned into crying and he went back to his room. His parents followed him. When Sean calmed down, he said, "Everyone expects me to do everything. I'm in the school play, I'm on the baseball team, I'm in the concert, I'm the editor of the school paper, and I have to make sure I can run the charity night well so we raise enough money to help buy a new wheelchair for Josh. I'm not a machine. I can't do it all!"

Sean's parents agreed with him. They talked about how Sean never focused on his feelings to know when he was starting to feel overwhelmed. He hadn't realized when he first started to feel unhappy and stressed. He admitted, "I probably would have asked for someone to co-run the charity night with me and I would have stayed as a reporter, not editor, for the paper if I knew it was going to stress me out so much."

- If you were Sean, would you have known that you were taking on too much before feeling overwhelmed?
- If you realized you were too stressed, how would your feelings have helped you?
- What would you have done?

Kids sometimes do things they don't feel good about to be accepted by friends, or they take on extra commitments because they want to please adults. They might not pay attention to feelings associated with peer pressure (like anxiety or discomfort), ignoring these important warning signs until they feel really uncomfortable or upset. They, like Sean, might commit to an activity because they didn't focus on the fact that they were already too busy. They might not even initially realize when they are having feelings of stress or are overwhelmed. If you are aware of your feelings, you might be able to find ways to reduce your stress level or ask for help when you need it.

When you are not sensitive to feelings, such as your sadness, fear, anger, or stress, you may not realize that something needs to change in your life. You may not always recognize what makes you happy either.

So, why is being aware of your own feelings important in becoming an Upstander? If you can identify your own feelings and know how to handle them, you may later know how to:

- look for early signs that another person may be stressed or upset;
- support someone who is upset, since you already developed these support strategies to help yourself;
- help another person realize that even uncomfortable feelings can be helpful in letting us know when we need to problem-solve or change a situation!

If you are aware of your feelings, you might be able to FIND WAYS to REDUCE YOUR STRESS level or ask for help when you need it.

BROOKE'S STORY

Using positive self-talk is important for yourself now and when you are trying to be an Upstander later. Brooke was extremely motivated to help others, but she wasn't very kind to herself. Brooke, age 10, told her parents, "I wish I could help everyone feel happy."

Brooke's goal was great, but before deciding if it was a realistic goal, her parents gave her a challenge. They asked her to first figure out how she could stop insulting herself and feel happier and more confident when taking on new tasks and experiences. Brooke accepted the challenge, thinking it would be easy to show her parents that she could be happy and not insult herself.

However, within two days, Brooke caught herself struggling in this area. She told her father, "I'm not going to the school dance because I'm terrible at dancing." Brooke's father explained to her that she was using negative, not positive, self-talk. She had been telling herself that if she tried a new activity and didn't immediately excel, that she deserved to feel embarrassed. Her father asked, "Is this what you want everyone else to do to themselves? Should people avoid taking healthy risks that might be fun and enrich their lives?" Brooke admitted that she felt better once she learned about positive self-talk. She told herself, "I'm actually gutsy for trying to dance. I can even find the courage to ask friends for tips on their dance moves. It might be fun!" Brooke learned that the skill of positive self-talk was important and that she wanted to share this skill with others.

- Do you sometimes insult yourself, such as by calling yourself "stupid"?
- If you were Brooke, what words would you have used if you thought you couldn't dance well?

Be Supportive
of Yourself

Do you often encourage yourself, or do you ridicule or criticize yourself? Being an Upstander should start with standing up for yourself. Remind yourself that you are a good person, that you can learn from mistakes, and that you can learn to be patient when you don't immediately succeed at something new or when trying to reach goals.

Positive self-talk is when you try to acknowledge your efforts and strengths, even while working on areas that may be hard for you. If you learn how to do this well, then you can be a role-model for others and even reframe your friend's negative self-talk.

Here are some examples of changing negative self-talk into positive self-talk:

Your art teacher looks at your watercolor painting and says, "You show promise and I'm glad you are trying. I'll be able to give you some great tips in this class."

- Negative self-talk: "I know my art teacher was actually thinking that my work stinks and I need lots of help."
- Positive self-talk: "I am proud that I had the courage to try a new activity. I don't need to be perfect and I am willing to learn new skills from my teacher."

You mispronounce a word while reading aloud in class.

- Negative self-talk: "I am so mad at myself. How can I be so stupid?"
- Positive self-talk: "I made a mistake and misread a word in class. Big deal. I thought it was funny the way it sounded, but I wasn't sure how to say it the right way. It doesn't mean anything, really, except that I need to learn the correct way to pronounce that word."

When it comes to using positive self-talk, always remind yourself that you are human and are going to make mistakes, so treat yourself with respect even when these mistakes occur. When you are open to trying new experiences, it's more fun if you don't expect yourself to be perfect; you can then be free to have fun and learn!

If you want to help people who feel down, you may want to teach them to use positive self-talk. Start with modeling it as you voice your thoughts about yourself. They (and you) may not be able to always control how the world treats them, but they do have control over how they treat themselves. Once you get used to using this skill, you may find yourself in a better place to teach it.

Cope With Frustration

Do you sometimes want to scream, kick, and give up? Life is filled with difficult moments—and it's okay to feel frustrated—but knowing how to calm yourself so you can handle the situation is important.

Sometimes people talk about using mindfulness, relaxation, or even yoga to help reduce feelings of frustration or to cope with being upset. Find what works for you and then remember to use it. Here are some tips:

- Learn how to recognize when you are upset or frustrated, so you know when to take a step back and reconsider the situation.
- A lot of problems don't have to be dealt with immediately. It's okay to take time to calm down before responding to others if you are really upset. For instance, you could say, "I need to think about this problem" or "I have to run right now. I'll get back to you."

- Tense then relax your muscles from your forehead down to your toes. Focus on one muscle group at a time. Start with crunching up your forehead, then relax it and move on to your cheeks or mouth and, eventually, all the way to your toes. This exercise could relax you enough to feel better able to deal with frustration.

- Use visual imagery and go to a calm place in your mind. The next time you have uncomfortable feelings or are feeling really stressed, close your eyes and imagine being somewhere that makes you feel calm or happy, such as at a recent relaxing vacation. Once you practice this a few times, it may only take a couple of minutes to realize that you are less stressed.

- Don't be afraid to ask for help if you are frustrated because you don't know how to handle a situation or you want guidance.

Achieving a large goal is rarely easy and generally requires time and effort. Scientists, for instance, dedicate years of their lives to developing cures for serious diseases. Even when frustrated and discouraged, they keep working if they feel that their goals are realistic and important.

If scientists gave up after their first few failed attempts, or if they yelled, cried, and lacked the patience to keep trying, think about how many cures and treatments would never have been discovered.

You may feel frustrated and disappointed when you think about all the problems in the world. Knowing that you are able to cope with frustrations can help you focus on how to handle seemingly overwhelming situations. If you can feel in control of your emotions, then you can begin to brainstorm realistic goals and make plans to reach them.

CONNOR'S STORY

Connor wanted to help kids struggling with hunger around the world. When he asked his parents for $100 to help him to get started, they said they couldn't afford to give him that much, but that they supported his goal and would give him a smaller contribution. Then they asked him what his plan was to reach his goal. Connor started yelling that they didn't have faith in him. He went to his room, slammed the door, and later decided not to focus on any part of his goal since he really didn't know how to accomplish it.

Connor struggled with three important skills:

- frustration tolerance (ability to tolerate some frustration);
- making a plan for reaching his goal (this will be discussed in Chapter 7);
- confidence that his goal was realistic and reachable.

- Do you think Connor could have responded differently to his parents?
- If you were in Connor's situation, how would you have reacted to the frustration he felt?
- Do you think Connor was right in giving up his goal?
- Connor had an important goal but wasn't sure how to reach it—could he have asked for help? If so, who could he have turned to for help?
- Do you have people who you turn to for guidance and support?

Develop Self-Confidence

If you want to work to make a difference in the world, you really do need a certain degree of self-confidence. Imagine if you doubted your abilities, questioned whether you had the confidence to tell others about your ideas, and worried that people would laugh at you if you asked for their help to reach your goals. You might never pursue a worthwhile goal because you didn't believe in yourself.

So, what is self-confidence? Self-confidence is when you know that you are capable, but you are also aware of your weaknesses or what you could work to improve.

Self-confidence is when you know who you are and feel proud of yourself and like yourself even though you are not perfect in every way (no one is, right?).

Self-confidence can give you the courage to stand up for others and take on challenges. It can also give you the courage to ask for help as you try to reach your goals. Did you know that asking for help when you need it is a sign of strength—not weakness?

Some people have pseudo-confidence, which means they pretend to be confident but feel insecure inside. People who do this could miss out on getting the help they need to really build their confidence, because others don't know that they even need the support to learn how to truly feel confident.

Pseudo-confidence sometimes leads to individuals acting arrogant, like they are better than others in what they know and can do, even though they are hiding insecurities. A person might do this if they can only feel good about themselves if they are number one.

What can you do if you aren't confident right now?

- Treat yourself with respect and use positive self-talk. Negative self-talk will only bring you down.
- Don't fall into the all-or-nothing trap. If you only feel good about yourself when you get a perfect test score or the Most Valuable Player award, then you are expecting

perfection and depriving yourself of the confidence that comes from putting in effort and improving skills.

- Focus on the glass being half full. If a glass is filled half-way with water, you can say it's half full or half empty—both are technically right. But if the water represents your talents or special skills and, rather than feeling proud of those, you only focus on the half-empty part, which represents what you can't yet do, it can hurt your self-confidence.

- Celebrate your courage to try safe, new challenges, even when you haven't been successful yet. Just be careful not to appear to brag while you are celebrating, of course.

- Don't only compare yourself to others—compare yourself to yourself. Set realistic goals and experience the pride that comes from moving closer to achieving them.

Kids watch other kids, which means kids may learn from watching you. Do you insult yourself when you don't achieve your goals? Or do you say, "I'm getting better, so that's good!"

Do you show your confidence by asking for help without feeling embarrassed? Even without specifically telling kids that it's okay if they are not perfect or they need help, you can teach them by being a role-model. Give it a try!

START SMALL!

When you catch yourself feeling frustrated, try using some of the calming strategies that you just read about in this chapter.

Look back on today. What happened that made you feel proud? Did anything happen that showed you an area that you might want to improve? If so, focus on the glass half-full method to remain confident while figuring out what to do to improve in other areas.

3

THE BASIC SKILLS
YOU NEED TO HELP OTHERS

NOW THAT YOU HAVE HAD THE CHANCE TO THINK ABOUT what kind of bystander you have been and the importance of self-confidence and being kind to yourself, let's look at some additional skills you can work on to help others.

This chapter will teach you how to support the other kids and adults in your life.

Even when you are focusing on helping others, you need to have fun, and sometimes you will need to put yourself first. It's great to help others, but you need to do it in a way that is comfortable for you and when it doesn't mean that you constantly miss out on other experiences that you value. It is not selfish to put yourself first sometimes.

This chapter focuses on developing skills like empathy, perspective-taking, altruism, the power of a smile, and kindness.

As you read about these topics, think about whether you can use these skills while still taking time for yourself.

Try taking the questionnaire on the next page to think about which skills you might need to work on. It's just a way to think about how much support you need in order to develop these skills, or to find out if you are already using them (although everyone could probably benefit from learning even *more* ways to use these abilities).

Quiz

1. When your teacher hands back test grades, you overhear a classmate, Andrew, say "I'm so depressed. I only got a 94." Then Andrew holds his head in his hands and looks down at his desk. Do you:
    a. roll your eyes, thinking, "He should get over it. He got a great grade"?
    b. try to imagine what it feels like to be Andrew, who is only happy with perfect test grades?
    c. reach out to him after class and try to help him, by showing him how you might use positive self-talk if you were disappointed with a grade?

2. Recently, a girl named Emma has been trying to hang out with you and your two close friends. Your friends have come up with a plan to avoid Emma. Do you:
    a. go along with the plan because it's better than directly telling Emma that you don't want her around?
    b. think about why Emma is trying to hang around you and how she might be feeling?
    c. try to help Emma feel included sometimes because you don't want her to be lonely and sad?

3. Maggie tries to pull a notebook from her desk and suddenly everything comes tumbling out. She scrambles to pick up her things, and a few kids point at her and laugh. Do you:
    a. look away from Maggie so she has more privacy to clean up?
    b. try to imagine how you would feel in Maggie's situation and wonder if Maggie feels the same?

c. think Maggie might be embarrassed when the other kids laugh at her, so you either try to help her pick up her things or tell the other kids that "It's really not a big deal"?

4. You see 6-year-old Nathaniel at the library with his mother. He is upset because his mother won't let him check out a chapter book that his older sister has just returned. Do you:
   a. feel annoyed that he's being so demanding and loud?
   b. try to imagine what it's like to be Nathaniel and too young to do the same things as his older sister?
   c. try to figure out how you can help? For instance, you may eventually ask the mother if you can recommend an age-appropriate book to Nathaniel that you, an older kid, think is great.

5. Brad is a friend of yours. He sometimes stutters and is really upset about having to give a presentation in front of the class. Do you:
   a. say that you love speaking in front of the class and suggest he will like it too?
   b. acknowledge his anxiety but also help him focus on the fact that he knows his material?
   c. acknowledge his anxiety, remind him of his well-organized presentation, and promise to smile at him to remind him that he has someone in the audience who is supportive?

If you answered mostly 'a', then you are likely beginning to understand the perspective of others and how they might be feeling. If you answered mostly 'b', then you are likely on the road to being empathetic and understanding of how others might feel. If you answered mostly 'c', then you seem to have an understanding of empathy and perspective-taking, as well as the power of being kind and helping others.

Skill Building

In the last chapter, you read about how some people may feel differently from you even if you are in the exact same situation. Everyone is an individual. It's part of what makes people so interesting.

Similarly, some kids—or even adults—may act or react differently from you in the exact same situation. This makes sense, right? However, figuring out what a person feels and why that person chooses to act in a certain way may take time and practice. Some people are easy to read: they cry when they are sad, pound their fists when angry, and verbalize their feelings most of the time. You may need to take more time and be more attentive to subtle cues, though, to understand other people.

You might be thinking that you're not a mind-reader. For example, how could you figure out what someone feels or why they are behaving the way they are if they don't tell you? This is an understandable reaction. Don't give up, though. By learning to take the perspective of someone else, having motivation to focus on how they are feeling, and being a bit of a detective, you may be surprised at how much information you can discover about what another person is feeling and needs!

Empathy

Empathy and perspective-taking are key skills to have when helping others. Empathy is generally defined as caring enough to try to put yourself in the shoes of others to see what they might be feeling and what they may want or need.

If you are empathetic—meaning that you have empathy and are trying to figure out how another person might be feeling—here are some things to consider:

- Look at body language. Did the person change eye contact (e.g., stare at another person or look away)? Did the person physically move away from others?
- Look at facial expressions. Sometimes people try to hide their emotions, but teary eyes, a clenched jaw, and reddening cheeks could be clues that a person is upset.
- Don't assume that the other person feels exactly like you would in the situation (for example, maybe that person feels teased or embarrassed by a joke that you would have found funny).
- Notice the people around you. Think about who is confident and who may need a friend. You may not always guess correctly, but it's good to think about who you might help to feel happier or more supported.
- Think about how you could let people know that you care (discussed later in this chapter).

Even while watching TV, you could build empathy skills by trying to figure out how the characters feel and why. It's not always easy to think about how others feel. Sometimes you may feel like you don't care—especially if you are in the middle of arguing with a sibling or friend. However, in general, if you want to change the world and be an Upstander, then you probably really do care about how others feel. Being sensitive to those feelings is an important first step in making an impact on those around you.

Perspective-Taking

Perspective-taking is closely connected to empathy. Empathy is caring about how someone feels. Perspective-taking, for the purpose of this discussion, is basically about trying to figure out how someone thinks.

STEPHANIE'S STORY

Stephanie, age 10, wanted to help all students in her school feel included and happy. So, she ran for student council vice-president. Her classmates, Elizabeth and Carly, were also running. When the announcement was made that Stephanie had won, she saw Elizabeth start to cry and leave the auditorium. Later, she overheard Carly tell her friends that she didn't really care because she was too busy to be vice-president anyway.

Later, Stephanie separately approached both Elizabeth and Carly. She told them they had great ideas during the campaign and asked if they wanted to help her make the school better by sometimes collaborating. Stephanie thought that she was being supportive and humble.

The two girls responded very differently. Elizabeth got mad and said, "First you steal the vice-presidency from me, and now you want to use my ideas and pretend they are yours!" Stephanie tried to be empathetic and imagine how Elizabeth was feeling. She realized that Elizabeth was both sad and angry about losing the election.

Carly responded to Stephanie by acting like she didn't even want to be vice-president to begin with, but she thanked Stephanie for reaching out to her. Stephanie understood Carly's perspective: she preferred privacy instead of publicly dwelling on the loss. Stephanie gave Carly space, but was still happy that she had reached out.

- How would you feel if you lost an election that you campaigned for and the winner complimented your campaign and asked to collaborate?
- If you were Stephanie, Elizabeth, or Carly, how would you have handled the news of who had won?

Perspective-taking skills can help you in all kinds of situations. Let's say that you are having a disagreement with a friend. Can you figure out what your friend's viewpoint is, even if you don't agree?

When you are arguing or you disagree with someone, it's helpful to take time to understand the other person's opinions. Here are some tips on how to do this:

- Stop, breathe, and try to relax so you can really listen to what the other person is saying.
- Try to restate your friend's viewpoint. Afterward, ask if you understood your friend's thoughts accurately or if you need help understanding.
- Carefully think about how you can respectfully offer your views.
- Encourage your friend to restate your point to make sure that both of you are communicating clearly, despite disagreeing.
- Try to figure out how important it is to your friend for you to be flexible and go along with her plan that day. If it's important, try to think about why, and if it's okay and safe for you to be flexible on that day.
- Think about whether you can find a way to negotiate and compromise so that both you and your friend are comfortable with how the conflict is resolved.

Imagine how different the world's history might be if people had always cared about one another's feelings and stopped to respectfully think about each other's opinions or perspectives. Could some wars have been averted? Could some marriages have been saved? If you care to develop empathy and perspective-taking skills, then you could make a difference in the world, one small step at a time . . . or maybe in a really big way. Congratulations for caring to learn these skills to help the world!

Altruism

. . . .

Altruism is basically wanting to help others because it feels like the right thing to do. It doesn't mean that you want to help someone out so that you get an award or money. If offered, it is okay to accept an award or money in certain situations, but if you are altruistic, then that wasn't what motivated you. You simply did it to help others.

Since you are reading this book, you are probably already altruistic. You probably already want to make the world a better place and to help people around you to be happy. When trying to be helpful, think about whether:

- your action will make the other person happy;
- your action may unintentionally embarrass someone;
- you should let the other person know what you did to help or if it's better to be kind but not mention it;
- you should check with adults before taking certain actions.

In some cases, even if you think you are being kind, your behavior might actually upset the person you were trying to help. For example, let's say that you purposely misspelled a word in the finals of the school's spelling bee because you wanted another student in your grade to win. You may have done this because you heard the other student studied really hard to win, she had never won anything else, and she doesn't have a lot of friends. You were trying to be thoughtful. There are many reasons why this isn't a recommended plan. Here are some of those reasons:

- It's okay to win the spelling bee if you really were the best speller that day.
- By purposely misspelling a word, you didn't allow the other contestants to have a fair competition.
- Other kids may realize that you purposely misspelled the word, and then tell your opponent that you would have beat her if you tried.

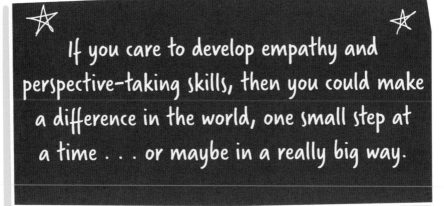

If you care to develop empathy and perspective-taking skills, then you could make a difference in the world, one small step at a time . . . or maybe in a really big way.

- The other student may feel like you were giving her charity rather than respecting her enough to win or lose based on skill.

Here are two more altruistic gestures that could lead to embarrassment or even resentment:

- You see that a classmate wears sneakers with holes in them, and that the other kids make jokes about how old the sneakers are. You do chores around the house to earn extra money, and then give it to that classmate to get new sneakers.
- You see that an overweight classmate eats high-calorie snacks each day. To help him lose weight, you offer to bring him fruit each day so he doesn't eat so many calories.

Can you see how these well-intended efforts could backfire and lead to more pain for the other student? The student may end up feeling embarrassed, self-conscious, like you are acting as though you are better than him, or angry that you are trying to help him when he didn't ask for, or even want, your help. Many people assume it's always good to offer to help others. However, how you help

ALEXANDER'S STORY

After a large snowstorm in his town, Alexander helped his family shovel their driveway and clean off their cars. After his parents gave him permission to try to help other families shovel out from this storm, Alexander immediately went to an elderly neighbor across the street, whose wife had recently died. Without asking, he shoveled the man's driveway and sidewalk. He then proudly rang the man's doorbell and announced to him, "I shoveled for you! I wanted to let you know that I care, so I did that."

The man offered Alexander money. When Alexander repeatedly refused to take it, the man seemed upset. Alexander was confused. When he returned home, his father told him that the neighbor had called. Alexander learned that the man felt like Alexander was doing charity because he viewed him as old. Alexander's father explained that sometimes neighbors may also feel uncomfortable if someone won't accept money. He added that while Alexander's behavior was very kind, he needed to always take the perspective of the other person and think about whether his action will be viewed as kind or as intrusive. His father told Alexander that the neighbor wants to give him money and that he should accept it.

In this case, Alexander learned that it would make the older man feel proud that he could pay him. Alexander went to the neighbor and graciously accepted the money. He then proceeded to send it to a food kitchen to help feed those in need.

- If you wanted to help neighbors by shoveling snow for them, how would you go about it?
- Would some neighbors be grateful while others might not be?
- Would you accept money if the person wanted to pay you?

and whether it will really be viewed as help are two key points to consider.

It can be helpful to talk with an adult before moving forward with an altruistic act. For instance, rather than giving an overweight student nutritious fruit or giving a child with worn out sneakers money to get new ones, an adult can let you know ways to be altruistic without causing embarrassment or other unwanted reactions.

Kindness

There are many things you can do to help others feel appreciated both at home and at school. Think about how it might feel if someone did these things for you. If you enjoy being kind to others, you may find that you feel proud of yourself when you engage in some of these altruistic (caring and kind) actions:

- Simply say please and thank you at appropriate moments to show respect for the other person.
- Write a letter to your parent, sibling, or other relative explaining why you value him or her. If you are allowed in that person's bedroom, it might be fun to put the note on his or her pillow as a bedtime surprise!

HELP OTHERS FEEL appreciated at home and at school.

- Have you ever heard the expression actions speak louder than words? Doing something kind is a great way to let some adults know that you care about them. Imagine how a parent might feel if you did an extra chore without being asked.
- You read this tip in Chapter One, but it's worth restating. If a classmate is out ill for a few days, send that person a quick text or e-mail (if you have access to this technology), or you can reach out with a quick phone call. It could help your classmate to feel appreciated and that you care enough to check in and see how he's feeling.
- If you have a relative who lives out of town, imagine how your relative might feel if you took the time to reach out? A quick phone call could lead to people feeling cared about and brighten their day.

This list consists of just a few ideas. In this chapter, the altruistic or kind acts listed are generally ones that you would do on your own. In later chapters, you will learn about activities to do with friends or siblings to help others.

The Power of a Smile

Imagine walking down the hallway at school, and a teacher or classmate smiles and nods at you. This small act would acknowledge that this person recognizes and is happy to see you. It would be a gift!

In Chapter One, you were encouraged to smile and say hello to a few other kids. Did you try it? If so, how did it go?

You may have already found out that if you smile and say hello to someone, that person is often going to give you the same gift and smile back at you! Smiles with different people may mean different things based on your relationship with them and whether there are words associated with the act. For example, if a person who always makes fun of Leah's clothing style smiles at her in the hallway and says, "Love that shirt . . . NOT!" this is clearly not a gift. In fact, some people would call it a smirk rather than a genuine smile. A smirk often implies that one person is laughing at the other, not appreciating her.

If you have a tense relationship with a classmate and suddenly start smiling at her, be sure that she doesn't mistake your smile for a smirk. Otherwise, your efforts to be caring could be seen as an attempt to make fun of, or even bully, her.

START SMALL!

1. Try to imagine how another person is feeling and what they are thinking in a particular situation. If it's someone you are close with, check to see if you are accurate. This activity can help you to build your empathy and perspective-taking skills.

2. Think about people who have inspired you. Next, consider if they would be embarrassed or happy (or even both embarrassed and happy) if you shared this with them. If you think it would make them happy, share it! If you aren't sure if they would be happy about it, check with an adult before you say anything.

4

KINDNESS AND ANGER
CAN BE CONTAGIOUS

YOU HAVE NOW READ ABOUT VARIOUS KINDS OF bystanders, how to be kind to yourself, and how certain skills (e.g., empathy) can help you to positively impact those around you. In this chapter, you will read about how your actions and how you display your emotions may impact those directly interacting with you and even people you don't know.

If you help one person to feel appreciated and happy, that person may be more patient and friendly with another person later that day. That third person, may also feel cared about and may then be more cooperative with her friends or parents! Because behaviors that can result from feeling happy (or upset) can impact one person, then another, and so on, we sometimes refer to this chain of impact as contagious. Feelings are not contagious in the same way a cold is, since people can decide to be caring even if they feel upset, but the fact that one's actions may impact another can be loosely described as contagious.

This chapter also covers the risks of stereotyping people. Have you ever guessed a classmate's interests and personality based on his clothes, or friends? Since you don't really know him, you may be making guesses or assumptions based on how his characteristics match those of a particular group. Of course, these assumptions may be right, but they may also be totally wrong.

Before reading this chapter, try taking the following question-naire as a way to think about which of the skills described are ones that you already have and use. This is just a way to think about how much support you need to develop these skills, or if you're already able to use these skills but may just benefit from some extra tips.

Quiz

1. When you are happy about something you did or something that happened to you, do you:
   a. tell lots of people about why you are happy, but forget to think about how they may react or feel about your news?
   b. feel so upbeat that you are less argumentative and more cooperative when asked to help out?
   c. love the feeling of being happy and want to help others to be happier by supporting them and helping them to feel appreciated.

2. You didn't get picked for the clarinet solo in your school's spring concert, even though you worked really hard. Do you:
   a. get mad and talk negatively about the music teacher and the person who got the solo, even though you know that the person is a more experienced clarinet player?
   b. question whether you are even any good at the clarinet and ignore kids who might benefit from your help?
   c. recognize that you are very disappointed, but still try to be altruistic because you know that helping others may actually help you (and the other person) to feel better?

3. A usually quiet kid is telling others in the hallway to move over, and he makes a negative comment about your hair. Do you:
   a. make fun of his shirt, thinking that he deserves the negative comment?
   b. you don't tease him back, but instead tell him that you didn't like the comment and continue walking with your friends?
   c. let him know you are worried about him because he's not usually insulting, and then ask if you can help him?

4. You see a boy, who is always sitting alone, picking his nose in the cafeteria. Do you:
    a. point out his behavior to your friends?
    b. try to start a conversation with the boy but abruptly walk away when he picks his nose again?
    c. let him know that it might be fun to play a board game together during indoor recess, but that you should both wash your hands so as not to spread germs?

5. You meet a distant cousin at a family get-together. Your mother asks you to talk with her. You notice that she dresses differently. You:
    a. think: I have nothing in common with her. I'll just say "hi" and move on.
    b. don't believe you have anything in common with her. You say "hi" and sit near her, but you don't talk directly to her.
    c. think that you may be very different, but you aren't sure. You sit down near her, and start talking. You are open to getting to know someone, whether you have some common interests or not.

If you answered mostly 'a', then you are likely starting the process of learning about how emotions, behaviors, and even stereotypes can impact the world around you.
If you answered mostly 'b', then you are likely on the road to self-monitoring and being open to being kind, despite days when you aren't feeling too happy or comfortable.
If you answered mostly 'c', then you seem to have self-awareness and know that it's okay to have whatever feelings you have, but you are already able to avoid spreading negativity through your behaviors or by stereotyping people.

Anger Can Be Contagious

Have you ever had a disagreement with a friend and it put you in a bad mood? Imagine yourself after that situation, still feeling angry and hurt. Would you have the same patience you often have with your little brother or sister if you are still upset when you arrive home?

One frustrating situation can lead to a person getting frustrated more easily in following situations. Clearly, this isn't the way that you want to impact the world.

ETHAN'S STORY

Ethan found out that his friend, Marc, invited two other friends to an amusement park to celebrate his birthday. Ethan felt angry and hurt that he hadn't been invited. He didn't ask Marc why he had been excluded. If he had, Ethan would have learned that Marc picked the other two friends because Ethan hated rollercoasters and that Marc was planning to invite Ethan and some other friends to his house for a small birthday party.

When Ethan got home from school, his anger and hurt feelings began to impact others. When his younger brother, Luke, started to tell him about riding a two-wheeler earlier that day, Ethan said, "big deal" without any enthusiasm. Luke, now, was feeling disappointed and frustrated. So, when Luke's twin brother, Danny, asked him to help with an art project, Luke said, "That's dumb" and walked away.

- How did Ethan's emotions and actions spread discontent, even when he was no longer involved in an interaction?
- If you were Ethan, could you calm yourself so that you don't spread negative feelings to others?

Remember these key points to stop this chain reaction:

- There are no bad emotions.
- You can feel uncomfortable but still treat others with respect.
- Try to learn from your feelings. For example, what is making you uncomfortable and what do you want to change?
- Anger and frustration do not control your behavior. You can still be an Upstander and a positive leader, even during difficult times.
- Be a role-model when you are upset to show those around you that people can still be caring, even when struggling with emotions like disappointment, anger, sadness, frustration, or anxiety.
- You can always ask an adult for help if you are upset and struggling to cope.

Kindness and Cooperation Can Be Contagious, Too!

Negative attitudes or actions can be contagious, but the good news is that the same is true for positive actions and words! Imagine finding out that you won your school's art competition—something you had been hoping for during the past few years—and that you would soon be competing against winners from other schools. You might feel really happy, smiling all day; you might even find out that others want to share in your good feelings. In addition, you might find that you want to help others to feel happy, so you are even more kind and helpful than on other days!

Do you think if other kids knew how to be altruistic and that it could be a positive experience for them, that they would want to

ALEXA'S STORY

Alexa won her school's art competition! She was having such a great day and felt so happy that she invited Jenni to join a discussion about an upcoming field trip. Usually Jenni kept to herself, and Alexa didn't bother reaching out to her. But that day, Alexa just wanted everyone to feel happy. After school, Jenni felt so pleased that she had been included in Alexa's conversation that she offered to help her sister with homework and to help her dad cook dinner. Jenni's sister and dad were so pleased with her behavior, that they were more patient and upbeat when they spoke to other people that evening. See? It's like kindness (and anger) are sort of contagious.

- Do you remember a time when you were feeling really happy and tried to share that feeling with others?
- If you were Alexa, and didn't want to brag, how would you share your good mood with others?

do it? If other kids don't notice that you are enjoying being kind, they may not focus on the power of supporting others. Sometimes, you may have to share your altruistic actions (without bragging, of course) to let others know how you feel after being altruistic.

Be a role-model to show how people can be altruistic. Altruism and kindness can be contagious only if others know how to do this. Here are some tips on how to teach others to be altruistic without being preachy or condescending:

- Could you write an essay for a class assignment about how famous people being altruistic has changed history? If so, could you share it with your classmates? There are many examples: Former presidents Bill Clinton

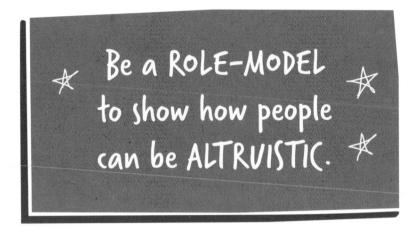

and George W. Bush have helped in Haiti. Bill and Melinda Gates have donated computers to schools and medication to third-world countries.

- Show people through your actions that you care about others, even when you aren't in the best of moods.
- Consider some of the group altruistic actions listed in Chapter 8 and try to include other kids from your school in the activities.

People who have positive energy (people focused on doing positive actions) are sometimes acknowledged throughout history. This can remind you that you are not alone in wanting to change the world. However, the world still has conflicts, bullying, and other difficulties. Perhaps your generation can start young and have major impacts!

Spreading Kindness

Once you identify a need, it's easier to come up with a way to help. There are lots of opportunities to be kind. You don't have to always focus on others to make a difference in the world. You just have to act like a detective, identify when someone around you needs support, and sometimes step in and make a difference for that person. Here are a few occasions when stepping in might help:

- A classmate seems confused about the homework assignment. Why not ask if he wants you to review it with him or even set up a study session?
- Your older brother is studying for a big test and your little brother is running around making lots of noise, making it difficult for your older brother to focus. Why not play a quiet game with your younger brother? By doing this, you would be helping both of your brothers!
- Your friend is carrying a lot of books and she drops them all on the floor. Why not help her pick them up?

If others see you helping and being kind to a variety of different kids, they may view you as confident and caring. You may build a reputation of having the confidence to stand up for others and for noticing and caring when someone needs help.

Once you identify a NEED, it's easier to come up with A WAY TO HELP.

SARAH'S STORY

When Sarah was in the fifth grade, she noticed a new third grader on the bus who looked scared and sat alone. Sarah tried to imagine how this young student was feeling, then left her own friends and sat next to her. The new student, Kelly, smiled with relief because someone was being nice to her. Sarah felt pride in having impacted someone else! Sarah learned about Kelly's interests and, the next day, she introduced her to several other third graders. Sarah returned to sit with her own friends and enjoyed periodically looking over at Kelly and seeing that she and her classmates were often talking and laughing together.

- Have you ever wanted to help a student who seemed to feel alone and lonely?
- How would you have handled things on the bus if you noticed that Kelly was new and sitting by herself?

Kindness Certificates

One fun way to be caring is to make "Kindness Certificates." You could even include your friends by asking them to help. Decorate an index card, or similarly sized paper, and write 'Thank you for being kind!' Then fill in the specific ways that a person was kind, sign the card, and give it to the intended person. Imagine how your grandparent, bus driver, waiter in a restaurant, or substitute teacher would feel if he or she received a Kindness Certificate! When you show your appreciation and see the tremendous impact it can have, it can be an amazing feeling.

If you want to give a Kindness Certificate to another child, make sure he won't wonder why you gave it to him. Be very specific about why you decided to give him this certificate. You don't want him to get the wrong idea, assuming you want to date him or embarrass him, or that you were being sarcastic or that you were surprised he was even ever kind until now.

If you give someone a Kindness Certificate and it works out, why not share your idea with others, even if they didn't want to join you initially? Some kids may want to enjoy the same pride that you experienced. In this way, you may have given out one Kindness Certificate, but you impacted many other people who may give out their own Kindness Certificates!

Other Ways to Show Appreciation

Kindness Certificates are just one way to help others realize that you appreciate their behavior or comments. There are many other ways to help people feel appreciated.

Here are some quick tips:

- Let a student know that you learned a lot from his presentation in class.
- Acknowledge a person who was kind to you by thanking him.
- Think about how you would like others to let you know that they appreciate you, then try using that action or statement directed toward others.
- Send a quick text or e-mail letting someone know that you appreciate something he or she did.
- Spend time talking with the person to show that you value her friendship.

Think about what you already do to show appreciation for others, then take a second to smile and appreciate your altruistic efforts. Next, try to generate more ideas for showing someone that you appreciate him or ways you can help others feel recognized for their positive actions.

Remember that kindness can be contagious. So, if someone was kind to you, and you care enough to acknowledge this, then you both may feel the power of sharing kindness and want to share it with even more people.

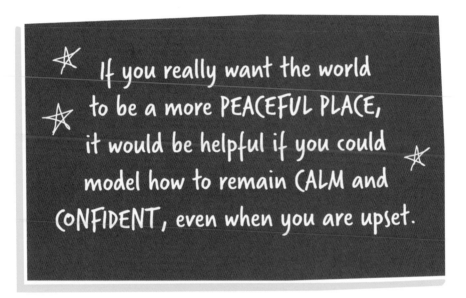

If you really want the world to be a more PEACEFUL PLACE, it would be helpful if you could model how to remain CALM and CONFIDENT, even when you are upset.

Staying Calm When You Are Angry

Kids may want to join in when you think of a kind and caring way to support others. However, if you show that you are only altruistic when you are happy—and that you can be very angry and disrespectful when you are not happy—your reputation and the message that others deserve respect at all times may be lost. Kids may also decide not to join you because they don't want you to disrespect them, even if it's only done rarely. If you really want the world to be a more peaceful place, it would be helpful if you could model how to remain calm and confident, even when you are upset.

TIMOTHY'S STORY

Timothy, age 10, initially had a tough time learning to remain calm and use positive self-talk. He admitted: "I used to get super annoyed at other people and even at myself when things didn't go my way. I used to roll my eyes at my parents and walk away from them, just because they wouldn't give me what I wanted. I told myself that I couldn't handle stress any other way. Also, when I had too much homework, I told myself and some of my friends that the teacher was 'mean' and, therefore, I shouldn't bother doing it. I am gradually getting better at positive self-talk and not losing my cool."

One day, Timothy's friend, Ryan, shared his thoughts about himself. He called himself "stupid" for missing free throws in a basketball game. Timothy told Ryan, "You need to be a better friend to yourself!" Ryan was confused. Timothy explained by telling Ryan he had a choice: he could get down on himself and call himself names or he could be nicer and use positive self-talk. Timothy told Ryan about how he's trying to figure out what he's really feeling, use positive self-talk, and then work on the issue rather than get mad at himself and at those around him.

Ryan agreed with Timothy. Why get so negative about your-self, especially when no one was purposely trying to be hurt-ful? Ryan and Timothy began to share their knowledge with friends. While a few kids thought the positive self-talk was "weird," many other kids began to try it. Yeah! They shared their knowledge of how to remain calmer even when disappointed!

- **Why do you think positive self-talk helped both Timothy and Ryan?**
- **Have you tried to calm down by using positive self-talk? If so, how did it work?**

Stereotypes Can Be Destructive

Did you know that stereotypes can also impact how people are treated? Stereotypes are assumptions that we make about people based on a group that they belong to or who they look or act like. Imagine meeting one kid from a foreign country and then assuming all others in that country are similar.

Could you be right? Perhaps in some ways and probably not in many others. For instance, the child's accent might be similar to others from that country. However, if you try to make guesses about likes or dislikes from this one person, your overgeneralization is likely wrong.

Stereotypes can lead people to pre-judge others based on limited information about them. The stereotype, even if positive, can hurt others. If a student who wears glasses and is on the debate team is viewed as smarter than others, that child may be expected to get better grades. The student may feel pressure because of this stereotype.

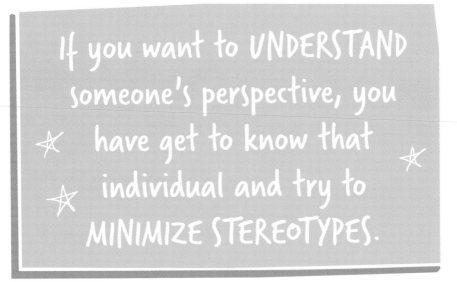

If you want to UNDERSTAND someone's perspective, you have get to know that individual and try to MINIMIZE STEREOTYPES.

Stereotypes can lead to:

- one group disliking an entire group of people based on an overgeneralization of information, assumptions, or inaccurate beliefs.
- quick guesses about who a person is, which can lead to major misunderstandings.
- people feeling misunderstood if others assume that they are similar to others with a similar characteristic.

Have you ever stereotyped a person? Stereotyping doesn't necessarily mean that you are cruel or trying to bully others. It may mean that you have to question your way of figuring out who people really are. If you want to understand someone's perspective, you have to get to know that individual and try to minimize stereotypes.

Here are some questions to ask yourself:

- Just because the new kid wears black a lot, are you right to assume he's part of a goth group? (Probably not—get more information.)
- Can you remember that everyone is an individual, it may take time to get to know others rather than stereotype, and that it's worth the time?

Have you ever been stereotyped? Maybe someone assumed that you were an athlete just because of your style of dress.

Things to consider:

- Do you think people in different countries or in different religious or racial groups stereotype each other? How do you feel about this?
- Do you think stereotypes help people to get along or do they keep people feeling very different so, therefore, they don't reach out to each other?

START SMALL!

Try letting two people know that you appreciate them. Be very specific about why.

Try to think of a group that is very different from a group you belong to. Perhaps it's a group of musicians in your school or kids who have a different skin color from you. Now, try to find three similarities between the members of that group and you. Thinking about this can remind you that human beings have many similarities, despite many different mindsets or cultures. It can also give you the foundation for connecting with others in these other groups by focusing on either the similarities or your interest in learning about some of the differences.

5

RESPECTFULLY DEALING WITH CONFLICTS

IT IS EXTREMELY RARE FOR ANY TWO PEOPLE TO HAVE
the exact same opinions and preferences every minute of every day
of every year. One of the great things about people is that we think
for ourselves and have our own viewpoints. However, this also means
that sometimes our opinions may conflict with someone else's.

If you want your opinion or preference to be heard over another
person's, it can be helpful to consider whether you need or just
want things to go your way. There is a big difference between
needing something to happen and wanting something to happen.
For instance, if you are diabetic and need to get medical treatment
because your sugar levels are very high (or low), it is truly a need.
You may want to be in class with your best friend, but you probably
don't need to.

How people deal with having differing wants is important; they
could try to work through a disagreement, negotiate, or compromise.
If you want the world to be more peaceful and for people to respect
each other, you can model this in how you deal with disagreements
or conflicts.

In this chapter, you will read about how you can respectfully share
your opinion and try to hear another person's viewpoint. Negotiation and compromise skills are important as you pursue your goal of
changing the world for the better.

Try taking the questionnaire on the next page as a way to think
about which skills you need to work on and which you already use
(but could possibly improve). It will give you a chance to think about
how you handle conflicts or differences of opinion.

Quiz

1. You feel strongly about what you and your friends should do this upcoming weekend. Do you:
    a. tell your friends what they should think and do?
    b. tell your friends what you think and listen to their views, but still try to convince them to follow your lead?
    c. tell your friends what you think, listen to their views, discuss the pros and cons, and try to compromise?

2. You are working on a group project in class, and one of the students doesn't want to go along with the plan the others in your group presented. Do you:
    a. get mad and tell this student to find another group?
    b. talk about how everyone needs to find a way to work together, even though each person may need to compromise a bit?
    c. talk about the issue and have everyone try to work it out, modeling how to use 'I' messages and be respectful?

3. A classmate purposely talks loudly, and always seems to comment that he has more fun, more friends, or higher grades than everyone else. Do you:
    a. decide to be honest and tell him, "You are so annoying?"
    b. think about why he behaves in this way, and then respectfully tell him when his behavior impacts you?
    c. compliment him on what you admire or like about him, but then politely remind him that having more fun or more friends or even higher grades sounds like a competition, but that you don't want to compete with him?

4. You have noticed that your friends use the word "bully" a lot. Anyone who disagrees with them or does something without thinking seems to get this label. When they call a classmate, who isn't always respectful, a bully, but you disagree, do you:

   a. ignore it? After all, what's the big deal if you think it is an exaggeration?

   b. casually say, "She's not always thoughtful in what she does, but I don't think she's a bully"?

   c. let your friends know that you think she isn't always the most respectful, but your definition of a bully is a bit different?

5. When you are in a conflict with your parents, do you:

   a. educate them on how you thought out your view and tell them that they should give in to you?

   b. give in to what they want to avoid a disagreement and because you always want to be respectful?

   c. have skills to talk about the issue and come to a resolution where you and your parents leave feeling heard and respected?

If you answered mostly 'a', then you are likely starting the process of learning about how to respectfully deal with conflicts and may pick up some important tips as you read this chapter.

If you answered mostly 'b', then you are likely on the road to developing conflict-resolution skills, but sometimes may not know the best way to handle a disagreement.

If you answered mostly 'c', then you seem to have some conflict-resolution skills, but may want to think more about this topic so that you can handle future disagreements.

EVAN'S STORY

Evan, age 12, learned that conflict can sometimes lead to positive changes. Evan shared a room with his 8-year-old brother, Benjamin. Benjamin loved to draw, but often drew on the back of papers that were important to Evan, such as homework assignments. Evan always talked about respecting others, yet he resorted to yelling and destroying some of Benjamin's papers when he was frustrated.

One day, Evan decided to try to resolve this conflict in a positive way. He sat down with Benjamin when they were both calm.

Evan told Benjamin that he really liked being with him and liked his artwork, but didn't want to argue so much.

Benjamin agreed that it would be good to stop the tension.

Evan explained how he felt when Benjamin drew on his papers. Benjamin said, he needs to draw when he feels like it.

Evan asked Benjamin if he was purposely trying to upset him. Benjamin said that he was not.

Evan then asked his mother if Benjamin could have sketchbooks. She agreed.

Evan offered Benjamin a sketchbook and the chance to pick his favorite picture every week to frame on their wall.

Benjamin stopped drawing on Evan's papers!

Benjamin felt like his artwork was appreciated. Evan felt like he and his brother grew closer.

- How would you have felt, both before and after his discussion with Benjamin, if you were Evan?
- How would you have handled the situation?

Conflict Resolution

There have been conflicts throughout history. People and governments may have different thoughts about how to handle situations. Having a conflict doesn't automatically mean that people will end friendships and countries will go to war. In fact, sometimes conflicts lead to honest, open discussions and positive changes!

Helping Others to Deal With Conflicts

Situations might be handled differently depending upon whether they are simple annoyances, peer conflicts, or situations that involve bullying. Let's look at each of these kinds of difficulties.

Conflicts happen. Disagreements happen. Imagine being a peace-maker, able to help others to work through these situations. Before you can become a peacemaker though, you will need to know:

- how strong everyone's feelings are about their point of view (sometimes one person may not even view the situation as a conflict);
- how long the situation has been going on;
- whether the people have entirely opposite views or if they are close to saying or believing in the same goal;
- if everyone even wants to work through the difficulty;
- if everyone wants you to get involved and help;
- what strategies they have already tried (so you don't repeat them).

Brief conflicts or issues may last only a few minutes and those involved may resolve the difficulty without anyone else's intervention.

For example, one student may run in the hallway and accidentally bump into a classmate. The person running may simply apologize, and the classmate may not harbor any negative reaction to this event.

These brief conflicts are also known as annoyances. An annoyance may lead to intense feelings, but for this discussion, it's generally not something that would often require a third party's help.

Some longer disagreements or conflicts also don't need a third party. Sometimes the people would rather deal with the situation on their own. However, at times, you may be able to help others resolve a disagreement or conflict if they are comfortable with your intervention. If you find yourself in this situation and you have answered the questions posed above, think about the following guidelines:

- Make sure that both people, and you, can devote some time to discuss the conflict and focus on resolving it.
- Set ground rules (e.g., respectful language; not talking over each other).
- Try to be objective and not biased toward one outcome or opinion (unless it's a safety issue, of course).

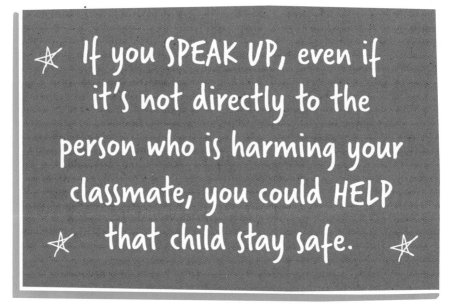

If you SPEAK UP, even if it's not directly to the person who is harming your classmate, you could HELP that child stay safe.

- Let the others know that you aren't taking sides.
- It can be helpful to let the others know that you might need similar help from them one day (so they know that you don't feel superior to them).

Once the ground rules are set for the discussion, it's time for you to focus on strategies for conflict resolution and for styles of communication that can help or hinder progress in your efforts.

Helping Others Deal With Bullying

Now that you have read about helping others to resolve conflicts, it's important to know that sometimes using these strategies may be neither appropriate nor effective.

Imagine a classmate in danger of being harmed by another kid. Imagine hearing that a child at school is being beaten by a family member. If you are an Upstander, should you step in and defend these kids?

Upstanders don't ever need to put themselves in harm's way. You wouldn't need to fight the bully or confront the child's family member in the above scenarios. There are things that you can do, though. Think about who you trust. If the situation is as serious as the two above, it's important to tell an adult. You might want to share the information with your parent, because it's often helpful to brainstorm how to proceed with adults you trust.

If the situation is happening to a student, try to think of an adult at school who might also help. Do you trust your teacher, your guidance counselor, the school social worker, or the school psychologist, for example? Ask them to try to keep your name confidential (that means private). Tell them as much specific information as you know, why you are worried for the student, and work hard to not present your theories as facts.

If you speak up, even if it's not directly to the person who is harming your classmate, you could help that child stay safe!

If you aren't sure if a person is really being bullied and whether you need to include an adult, ask yourself the following questions:

- Does one person have more power than the other person in the situation?
- Does one person act aggressively (either physically or verbally), intending to harm the other person?
- Does this happen repeatedly or intensely?

If the answer is yes to these questions, then assume that the situation might involve bullying. It would definitely be time to seek help to figure out what the best way would be to handle the difficult situation.

Passivity, Aggression, and Assertiveness

Let's go back to things you can do to be respectful, share a positive attitude, and to be a role-model for how to handle disagreements with others. In general, there are three different ways people can handle situations. One person could use any of the three ways, depending on the situation. Another person might stick to one style of communication, no matter what the specific situation is that they are encountering.

As you read about the terms and general definitions, think about whether you are usually in one of the categories or switch from one to another. Here are the three general styles of communication:

- Passive—a person who is passive may try to avoid conflicts, even to the point of being seen by peers as a pushover. He doesn't stand up for himself and defers to others.
- Aggressive—a person with this communication style does not necessarily become physically aggressive, but may loudly convey that her needs are more important than another person's. She may even talk negatively about another person. She may not be a bully, but she can be hostile when others are trying to open lines of communication.
- Assertive—a person who is assertive is respectful of others but also wants to stand up for what he believes in. He tries to avoid insulting others or devaluing an opinion that differs from his own. He seeks resolutions to conflicts that seem acceptable, but his goal is not to just 'win' over another person.

People also talk about a passive-aggressive style of communication, which is a blend of the first two styles listed above. A person communicating passive aggressively may withdraw but, in doing so, can end up manipulating another person to the point of that person feeling upset or inconvenienced. He may be passive-aggressive when "forgetting" to give the other person an important message because he's angry about a previous situation, for example.

So, have you determined which style you usually display? There may be times when you are frustrated or upset with how another person is treating you. Making a difference in the world doesn't mean letting others always do what they want and never feeling angry. It just means that you know how to be assertive rather than aggressive or passive so that your needs can be met and you don't purposely set out to be disrespectful.

Clear Communication Strategies

There may be times when you are upset with someone's comments, behaviors, or decisions. Here are some tips for dealing with conflicts (when no bullying is occurring). These ideas might help you as you try to assertively communicate with that person and model adaptive conflict-resolution skills:

- Calm down before talking about the issue at hand.
- If you are too emotional to listen and respectfully share your views, pick a later time to talk.
- Avoid having an audience around when you talk to the other person. Others might take sides or the person you are talking to might feel that it's important not to back down from an opinion in front of her friends.
- Ask the person if it's a good time to talk about the situation. If it's not, ask when there is a good time.
- Let the other person know that you are upset, but (if it's genuine) that you do admire some of his abilities or skills (be specific).
- Together decide who talks first. When the other person talks, try to really listen carefully to what she is expressing.
- Try to summarize the other person's point of view to make sure you heard it correctly. This will also show the other person that you truly did hear his message.
- Ask the person if you accurately summarized what he said and, if not, ask what you missed. This shows you really care!
- When it's your turn, share your viewpoint with clear, respectful language. Remember that it's okay to be assertive, but aggression can complicate things.
- If you aren't sure how to share your opinions, try using an 'I' message (you will read about this in the next section).

- Ask the other person to restate what she heard you say. If your message wasn't heard clearly or fully, acknowledge what was clearly heard and then calmly and respectfully add what you felt was missed.

Even if you use these strategies, the situation may not get resolved. However, you both may have a greater understanding of the other person's thoughts and feelings. You may need to agree to disagree or you may eventually come up with a compromise.

Sometimes, people will not change no matter how hard you try to change them. For instance, your parents may feel strongly that you shouldn't go to a friend's party if no parent is going to be home. Even if you disagree with this parental decision, you can know that you tried to discuss it, heard your parents' viewpoint clearly, and will just have to deal with it.

At the start of this chapter, you read a bit about needs vs. wants. If you have a true need, keep talking until you find someone who can help you to reach your goal. Remember, needs are serious. If you don't get your need met, something bad is likely to happen. A want may be something you can get later or not at all.

You may try to calmly get what you want, but sometimes you may end up not getting it. If you can accept that you may feel disappointed, but that nothing terrible will happen if you don't get what you want, then you can be a great role-model for others who may not have developed this acceptance and may, instead, act out due to the frustration.

If more people could accept that human beings sometimes have different opinions, may disagree, and obstacles may occur, without yelling or hurting others (verbally or physically), wouldn't the world be more peaceful? You don't always have to accept the status-quo if you feel that you have an idea for improving a situation. However, accepting that others may not be convinced that you are right, and remaining calm, allows you to try again another day, perhaps in another way!

The Power of
'I' Statements

'I' messages or 'I' statements are often a great way to try to make sure that you are not starting off a conversation in an accusatory or aggressive way. Unfortunately, many people (both kids and adults) use the word "You" when they start discussing disagreements. The sentence may be, "You don't understand," or "You haven't really thought this through," or even "You don't know what you are talking about!"

How do you think the other person might feel if you started a conversation with one of these "You" sentences? How would you feel if someone started talking with you about a disagreement using one of these sentences? Starting discussions in these ways can create tension without resolving the conflict.

'I' messages focus on you sharing your feelings with someone else, without accusations. In fact, feelings are feelings and not good or bad. 'I' messages start with an honest sharing of these feelings. Here is a general formula for 'I' messages (you may change it a bit to fit your style or the situation, of course):

I feel _____

because _____

when _____

I want _____

Remember: these messages are supposed to be free of judgements, accusations, and, of course, threats.

HERSHEL'S STORY

Hershel, age 11, tried out an 'I' message. He wanted to raise money and donate it to an organization that builds school buildings in countries that lack places for children to learn. Hershel's father was a hat designer and owned a factory that produced the hats. Since Hershel's father loved that his son was trying to help others, he agreed to make hats with Hershel's school's logo on them at a very discounted rate. Hershel hoped to sell lots of hats at school and donate the profits.

At school, Hershel was upset when his principal wouldn't let him set up a table to sell the hats the following week. Hershel tried to remain calm and set up an appointment to speak with the principal, Mrs. Moskowitz. At that meeting, Mrs. Moskowitz calmly explained that any use of the school logo must first be approved by the Board of Education in their school district.

Hershel decided to use a short and clear 'I' message. He said, "I feel frustrated because I'm trying to help kids and hoped the school would help. I want to find a way to do this now so the schools can be built and kids can learn." Mrs. Moskowitz, impressed by Hershel's style of communicating and altruistic goal, agreed to work with Hershel to ask the Board of Education for permission to proceed. Whether Hershel was given permission or not, he felt proud that he used the 'I' message and his principal responded positively to it.

- Have you ever wanted to reach a goal and felt frustrated when there was a roadblock?
- How did you feel?
- How did you handle it?
- Do you think that an 'I' message would help at these times?

> "I" MESSAGES or "I" STATEMENTS are often a great way to try to make sure that you are not starting off a conversation with someone else in an accusatory or aggressive way.

Negotiation and Compromise

Individuals and countries sometimes disagree. When a friendship ends or a war breaks out, it means that other kinds of conflict resolution have failed. Is it better to get some of what you want and let others get some of what they want rather than ending a friendship or countries going to war?

If you answered 'yes' to this question, then you may want to consider how you can negotiate and compromise during times of conflict. Negotiating really means communicating that you're willing to compromise.

There are certainly times when you shouldn't negotiate and compromise. As you read earlier, if you have a serious need, it must be met without compromise.

If compromising makes sense as a way to work through a disagreement, maybe you and the other person can brainstorm possible compromises together. Be creative.

ANGELICA'S STORY

Angelica and her mom compromised successfully. Angelica wanted to go to a friend's party, while her mom had decided that the whole family would spend that day celebrating a cousin's high school graduation. Their compromise was for Angelica to join the family celebration for two hours. After that time, Angelica's father agreed to drive her to her friend's party. Angelica wasn't at her friend's party for the entire time, which was her original goal, but she and her parents were comfortable with this compromise.

- Have you ever compromised?
- How did it feel?
- Did you feel like you gave in too much?
- Did you comfortably achieve what you really wanted, even though you didn't get everything you wanted? If so, that's great! You are learning important skills to get along with people and even work with others toward a common goal.

Ask for Help

There are times when adult support can lead to some very creative interventions. Clearly, as stated earlier in this chapter, dangerous situations should be reported to adults to assure that everyone is safe. However, there are other times when adults may be able to help you plan an event that can decrease peer conflicts.

LUIS'S STORY

Luis, age 11, wanted the kids at school to get along, even if they were in different groups. When he tried to tell the kids not to tease or insult each other, they sometimes teased and insulted him. Luis was frustrated and felt that as just one person, he was not able to change how kids treat each other.

After much thought, Luis decided to talk with his teacher about his feelings. His teacher thought his goal was great but his plan might need to be changed. With the help of the school's principal, Luis and his teacher planned a competition day at school, where kids were assigned to groups and had to figure out how to solve a variety of math problems, science games, and crossword puzzles. With Luis's help, the principal set up groups where kids from different social circles had to work together.

The sixth graders gathered in the gym and learned what they were going to be doing. They were told that the group that completed the most challenges in the shortest time would get a homework pass for an entire week. The kids were clearly excited. However, when they went to the bulletin board to find out who was in their group, some of the excitement was lost.

Luis then thought that the day was going to be awful. However, when the games began, the kids seemed to be working together to complete the tasks. Several hours later, most of the kids were laughing with the rest of their group! By the end of the day, many kids gained an appreciation for those who are different from themselves. They learned that even if they aren't friends with some students, they may still be able to find their positive qualities. These kids were truly the winners!

- Do you have a goal similar to Luis?
- If so, who could help you achieve it?

START SMALL!

Think about your last disagreement. Do you think that you could have come up with a way to negotiate and compromise rather than argue?

Think about yourself. Do you have a passive, aggressive, or assertive communication style? If you know of situations where you weren't assertive, try to role-play (in your head) how you might have handled the situation assertively. This can help you practice the skill of assertiveness before you need to use it again in the future.

CHANGING PATTERNS, CHANGING RULES

DO YOU ALWAYS AGREE WITH THE RULES YOU ARE ASKED
to follow? Sometimes you may notice rules that you disagree with and want to change. These rules may be fair but annoying, or they may be truly unfair. There are also clearly stated rules (e.g., you shouldn't cheat while taking a test), but there are many other agreed upon informal rules (e.g., ones that a group of friends follow, even if they are not clearly described to be rules).

In this chapter, you will get a chance to think about rules and whether they should be changed or kept as they currently are.

In past chapters, you learned about ways to handle conflicts respectfully. These skills are important as you try to decide whether you want to change longstanding rules.

You may upset people who like the rules, get resistance from people who don't like change, or personally face frustration when it turns out that it's difficult to change the rules. At these times, having problem-solving and conflict-resolution skills, as well as patience, can certainly be helpful!

Take a moment to complete this questionnaire, which focuses on the rule or behavior pattern that people may have around you, how you deal with it, and how you feel about it. For each situation, decide which of the three reactions is most similar to how you would respond.

This questionnaire can give you the opportunity to think about how you feel about and deal with rules, whether they seem fair or unfair to you.

Quiz

1. You feel it is unfair that you have to get dressed up for your middle-school graduation ceremony. Do you:
   a. agree to get dressed up, but right before the ceremony switch clothes?
   b. speak with the school principal and respectfully express your frustration, but then not listen to his perspective since you are sure that he is wrong?
   c. speak to the school principal, respectfully express your frustration, then listen to his perspective because you are open to reconsidering your stance?

2. Your friend feels that the world should have no rules, so she often does not follow rules if she disagrees with them. Do you:
   a. love that your friend is a rebel and follow her lead since she seems so confident that she should have no limits?
   b. follow your friend and break rules when you feel that they are unfair but follow the rules that you agree with?
   c. caution your friend when she is trying to break rules that could affect her safety, but talk with adults about why some rules should be followed even if safety is not an issue?

3. A popular kid in your grade always sets the rules for who people should talk to or ignore. You want to be popular. Do you:
   a. decide to ignore some students if the popular kid is nearby?
   b. try to change the topic when the popular kid sets these rules because you are uncomfortable leaving others out?
   c. feel that you would rather not have the popular kid as your friend if you must hurt the feelings of others, so you don't follow the rule of exclusion?

4. Your parents have a rule that no one can go on their electronic devices until homework is done. You don't like this rule, so you:
   a. close the door to your room and go on your device any time you want.
   b. try to suggest a replacement rule, such as that you can go on your electronics anytime as long as you get good grades.
   c. set up a time to calmly speak with your parents, ask them why they have the rule, then share your thoughts. You look for a compromise together.

5. You notice a lot of kids only hang out with people who look like them. You don't like this behavior pattern. You decide to:
   a. ignore it. After all, what can you do to change a situation that effects so many kids?
   b. try to get to know a few kids from different groups. You change your own behavior.
   c. try to understand why this occurs, then try to find someone in another group who also wants to change this pattern, and begin talking to your friends about it.

If you answered mostly 'a', then you are likely starting to learn about ways to deal with rules that you dislike, or even behavior patterns or rules that you feel are unfair.
If you answered mostly 'b', then you are likely learning to think about ways to calmly respond when you don't like rules or behavior patterns.
If you answered mostly 'c', then you seem to have self-awareness and know that it's okay to brainstorm ways to respectfully respond to rules that are not healthy, kind, or don't make sense to you.

Fair or Unfair Rules

It's important to think about the rules that you follow and whether they are fair. Sometimes we follow along and don't think much about rules until they personally upset us. Some rules may not upset you, but they may be unfair to some individuals. Other times, a rule may upset you, but there are good reasons to keep that rule in place. Confusing? Read on.

Rules have been written and then rewritten and changed throughout history. For instance, Malala Yousafzai became a teen activist because she was upset that girls weren't allowed to attend school in Pakistan. She even won a Nobel Prize recognizing her attempts to change this situation. Martin Luther King, Jr. was a leader who pointed out the need for racial equality and that rules regarding race (e.g., bus seating based on skin color) must be changed.

Can you think of any other examples from what you learned already about people in history who took a stand to change rules that they felt were unfair? What about people who changed the rules in a way that ended up hurting large groups of people? For example, the Nazis followed guidelines that Jews (and members of several other groups) should be removed from society and put into concentration camps. Many countries worked together to end the Nazi control and the discrimination against these groups. You may say that people in these countries became Upstanders who took a stand against this Nazi "rule," because they decided to help others living in their own or even faraway countries.

Sometimes it takes large groups of people to make major changes. The changes you make today may seem small by comparison to those mentioned above. However, no positive change is minor or small. Pick a change that you feel is important in the world, think about whether there is a way for you to pursue your goal, see if you can get others (including some adults) to join you in your efforts, and smile when you notice that change has occurred.

First, you should think about the rule that you are focused on changing or keeping. There are several different ways that you could view rules; let's look at three typical ways:

- **Appropriate, Comfortable, and Fair**
  In this case, you may just acknowledge the rule and agree that it is helpful for everyone to know the expectation since it is fair and comfortable. There are many rules that you need to follow that are fair. Even adults have rules that fall into this category, such as stopping their car at red lights. This rule was designed for the safety of all who drive, walk, or even ride bikes on the road, right?

- **Upsetting but Fair**
  These rules may annoy you, even though you understand why they are in place. For instance, you may love roller coasters but find out that you are not allowed to ride one because of the height requirement. This rule was designed to keep people safe and, once you think about it, you probably don't want to change it.
  If your parents set up the rule that no one brings their phone to the dinner table—unless your parents are dealing with an emergency—this may upset you. You may want to keep in touch with friends. However, if the rule is for everyone, and the goal is to have family time without distractions, you may have to accept this rule despite being upset.

- **Upsetting and Unfair**
  These are rules that seem illogical or unfair to you. When you notice one of these rules, you might want to work to change it. Perhaps there is a school rule that only those

who have been in band for one year can try out for a solo for the concert. You feel that this is unfair because you have been practicing a lot and believe that you are ready for a solo. However, you have to be open to the fact that there may be a reason why this rule is in place, that it's actually not harmful, and that it applies to everyone so all have equal treatment. Gather information before deciding that a rule is truly unfair.

When considering a rule, first determine which kind of rule it is, then decide whether you should put in the energy and time to challenge it. There are some societal customs, or behavioral rules, that are not meant to be discriminatory but rather to show respect. In these situations, you may not want to challenge the rules even if you don't enjoy them. For instance, in some cultures, bowing lower than another person, averting eye contact, or maintaining eye contact are customs that have a social message rather than being negative against a group.

You Have the Power to Change Some Unfair Rules

If you have identified a rule that you feel is unfair, ask yourself if you think you truly can change it. After all, can kids really make a difference in the world? Yes, they can when they set realistic and clear goals. Before trying to change the rules, though, there are some important things you should spend time thinking about:

- Why was the rule created in the first place? Get as much information as you can to understand this.
- Why has the rule continued?
- Does anyone or any group benefit from the rule?
- What positive or negative results could occur if the rule is changed?

GLORIA'S STORY

Gloria, age 13, was upset that her teachers ate in a different cafeteria, separate from students. When she complained about this rule to her parents, they suggested that she spend time doing some research and thinking about why this rule is in place.

Gloria did an investigation. She found out that the teachers have had a separate cafeteria since the school opened 30 years ago. She then asked some of her teachers about whether they liked this separate eating situation. All of her teachers said that they liked it, but that they would be glad to sometimes eat with the students in the student cafeteria.

Gloria tried to figure out if the teachers benefitted from this situation. She learned that the teachers have the same food choices, utensils, and trays as the students. However, the teachers often talk about lessons, share information about tests they are using, and support each other as professionals. Gloria then thought about the students' perspective. She was surprised to learn from other kids that they like having their own private time to talk without a teacher right there listening.

Gloria was happy that she did her investigation before challenging this situation. She learned that both students and teachers were treated equally and that everyone benefitted from separate cafeterias. Therefore, she decided to focus on inviting some teachers to the student cafeteria at pre-arranged times. This seemed to benefit both teachers and students.

- Would you have taken the time to do the investigation that Gloria did before setting a goal?
- How would you have handled this situation if you initially thought it was unfair?

Carefully think about whether a rule is truly unfair or just feels unfair. After all, if you put in the energy to set a goal and then try to achieve it, why not make sure that it's a goal worth pursuing?

What You Need to Know When Setting a Goal

In the next chapter, you will read about how you can try to make changes in your world. But first, it's important to set a realistic (achievable) and specific goal. A realistic goal is one that you could possibly achieve, even if the likelihood is small. For instance, perhaps you feel it is unfair that sometimes you have tests for two different classes on the same day. Your goal could be for each teacher to have an assigned day of the week for testing. Is this realistic and achievable? It might be. It might not be. You won't know until you pursue it. However, if your goal is that all students who try out end up getting a spot on the Varsity Football team, that may be unrealistic, because kids who are not physically skilled or able to play at a certain high level might get hurt.

When you set a goal, try to be as specific as possible. If you let other people know that you are going to "make the world fair," they may like the concept but won't know what you are actually going to do. It's great to have these general goals, but then you should take time to be specific about what you want to focus on at each step. Think about what the immediate goal is, the short-term goal, and then the long-term goal.

For instance, if you want teachers to give tests on different days, your immediate goal could be to have conversations with your teachers and even the principal to gain information. You may be able reach an immediate goal pretty quickly! The short-term goal might be to let teachers know when there is overlapping testing on a single day to see if they would consider changing their test date. The long-term goal might be to have a set schedule (probably set up by the principal) for when the English teacher, Social Studies teacher, Science teacher, and Math teacher can give tests. The long-term goal requires patience and motivation to respectfully work to achieve it.

Sometimes people get frustrated with a rule when it inconveniences them. Did your parents say that you couldn't go to a concert on a weeknight? Perhaps you are upset or frustrated, especially if your friends are going to the concert. But if your parents said you could go to the concert over the weekend, and you have a friend who wants to go then too, would you really want to challenge their rule? Maybe not. Also, if you are motivated to change a rule that is unrealistic to have changed, and the rule is not really unfair as much as annoying, maybe it's time to think about how you can deal with this frustration rather than working to change the rule.

Improving the Lives of Others

When kids set out to change the world, they are often motivated to increase kindness and peace. If this is your goal, know that achieving it can be difficult, but you don't have to do it on your own.

For right now, just think of a realistic immediate goal toward achieving a world with more kindness and peace. Remember reading about the Kindness Certificates? If your goal is to highlight others' acts of kindness, then you could be meeting your goal simply by giving out these certificates.

Adults and kids alike may truly love getting "caught" in an act of kindness by you, as long as they don't feel judged or that you are acting superior to them by deciding if they are kind or not. If giving out a Kindness Certificate reminds people that you value their altruism, perhaps they will be motivated to do even more kind acts! If this is the impact you have on others, even though it's not specifically a rule that you are changing, you are impacting the world.

Your Response
to Roadblocks

How you pursue your goals and how you handle setbacks are likely equally important. Imagine if your goal was to compete in the Olympics, but in a local competition you had a meltdown, crying and yelling at the judges when you didn't come in first place. Do you think this behavior would make you a good representative for your country, considering that you could receive a bronze medal instead of the gold or silver . . . or no medal at all? Do you think your teammates would feel that you were supporting them if you were only happy if you beat them?

If you are respectful of others, acknowledge their positive efforts and accomplishments, and don't expect everyone to always applaud your goals, then you are more likely to gain the support of others.

If you really want others to listen to your rationale for setting your goal, support you, and maybe even help you, here are some tips:

- Stay calm (getting angry may lead others to resist your idea and goal).
- State your goal clearly. Why do you want to achieve your goal? What are the pros and cons that you have already considered?

JASON'S STORY

Jason, age 11, felt that students would be less stressed and better able to concentrate in class if they had longer recess periods each day. He knew he would be happier with longer recess periods, but he truly believed that all kids could benefit from it.

Jason asked a few students if they agreed with his goal. With a few exceptions, the kids agreed that they would like to have more time outside at recess. On the rare occasion when a student disagreed with Jason's goal, Jason got angry and even once said, "Are you a kid or a robot? What's wrong with you?"

When Jason later asked some of his classmates to come with him to the principal to talk about extra recess, some of them decided they didn't want to join him because they were upset that he tried to force kids to agree with him. When he talked to the principal and the principal explained why recess was set for the time that it was, Jason told him that he wasn't really caring about the kids.

Ultimately, Jason lost some support from other students, and the principal assumed that he was simply trying to get out of school work. Jason never calmly and respectfully shared his rationale. He also never worked on alternative ideas to reduce student stress levels.

- How would you have handled Jason's goal?
- How would you have felt if you hit a roadblock, and it didn't look like you could reach your goal at that time?

- Be patient (change often does not occur instantly).
- Give others a chance to think about your suggestion.
- Offer a compromise if you think it could help you to get closer to your goal.
- Listen to others if they suggest another way to reach the same goal.
- Be respectful.

Think about how the world would be if people handled conflicts or obstacles respectfully. Do you think more world leaders would be open to talking and, hopefully, finding a way to co-exist without conflict? Why not start today by being a role-model for how you can deal with roadblocks or obstacles when trying to reach goals that others may not always support?

Being Okay With What You Can and Can't Change

Earlier in this chapter, you read about setting realistic and reachable goals—but this isn't always easy to do. Imagine if people never thought that women should vote in America? Imagine if people never believed that apartheid in South Africa could end? Imagine if scientists never believed that it was realistic to work to cure certain diseases?

Sometimes it's important to believe in ideas even though others feel they are impractical or unrealistic. Maybe you will surprise everyone and achieve your goal! Imagine how that would feel. However, if your goal is very large, you probably need to accept that reaching it will take time and hard work, and it could be frustrating. Set smaller goals and see if they are realistic. If so, continue working to reach larger goals. If they are also realistic, maybe the goal that others might have labeled as unrealistic may be reachable after all!

BE PATIENT.
Change often
does not
occur instantly.

Here are some tips to avoid major frustration:

- While setting large goals, also set smaller goals (immediate and short-term), so you have milestones to hit along the way.
- It may be okay, for now, to just educate others about your goals. They might want to help you achieve them to make the world better.
- Remind yourself that no one can create a world everyone feels is "perfect," so listen and learn from others rather than just getting upset if they disagree with you.
- Think about your behavior and your words, which you can control. What can you accomplish—by how you behave or what you say—to make the world better today?
- Learn about mindfulness, meditation, and relaxation exercises if you tend to get frustrated easily.

> **BE PROUD of your efforts and know that any time you CHANGE a truly unfair rule or group behavior pattern, you are making a DIFFERENCE.**

There are some rules that you may not be able to change; focus on the rules that you can change soon. Be proud of your efforts and know that any time you change a truly unfair rule or group behavior pattern, you are making a difference. Look around you. Look at your school and how kids treat each other. Who may feel better because you spent time getting to know them and highlighted a rule of inclusion? Even if your efforts to be kind aren't always met with positive results, you are likely to find that most people like to be acknowledged, such as by someone saying "Hi" to them or including them in activities or discussions.

START SMALL!

Think about a goal you might have for how you behave or talk with others. Can you identify an area that you might want to change, for yourself, that might lead you and others to feel calmer or more peaceful?

Look around your home, school, and community. Can you think of something that you might want to change (e.g., a rule or a way that people treat each other) so that people would feel more comfortable or respected? If so, write it down. In Chapter 7, you will read about the next step.

7

MAKING A PLAN AND
WORKING TOGETHER

HAVE YOU THOUGHT OF A REALISTIC AND SPECIFIC GOAL that you want to reach? If so, you have already taken one of the hardest steps. This chapter will take you through other steps needed to succeed—whether your goals are large or small, easy or hard. Interestingly, these same steps can also help you target everyday goals.

Some goals are quick and don't need a detailed plan. For instance, if you want to say hello to the new student today, you just need to remember to do this when you happen to see her. If you want to get to know her, you may want to plan a bit to figure out what questions you can ask without seeming intrusive.

Knowing what your goal is and deciding how to go about reaching it requires different skills. You may already have some of these skills, such as perseverance (to stay motivated and keep working), organization (to make a plan and then follow it to reach your goal), and initiation (knowing how to get started). If you don't have these skills yet, this chapter can help guide you to develop them.

Do you have a goal that could be hard to pursue? If so, the words of Mark Twain might inspire you: "The secret of getting started is breaking your complex overwhelming tasks into small manageable tasks, and starting on the first one."

This questionnaire on the next page is just a tool for you to gain a greater understanding of yourself. No matter what answers you have now, it does not mean that you will automatically struggle, or not struggle, when you want to make changes in your world. Once you learn some of the tools outlined in this chapter, however, you may feel more equipped to move forward.

Quiz

1. The end of the school year is approaching, and so is your science final. The test will cover everything you learned in that class during the year. Do you:
   a. glance at your binder that contains your notes and at the science book, then get so nervous that you think: I'll fail, so why even bother studying?
   b. feel unsure about how to even get started with your studying, but then get help from your parents and study with them each night until the date of the test?
   c. know how you remember things best and, therefore, decide to study all of the topics, one each night, until the date of the test?

2. In an online chat, you and your friends come up with a great new toy idea. You all set a time to meet and talk about how to create and sell it. At the meeting, you:
   a. realize that it's going to be a lot of work to get the materials, make the game, try to sell it or try to contact a big company to buy your game from you, so you say, "It's not really something I want to do. It seemed more fun when we were just talking."
   b. feel a bit overwhelmed with all the work, but decide to stay involved because one of your friends is super organized and agreed to outline the steps needed to try to reach your shared goal, and your other friend is super excited and keeps you motivated;
   c. realize that the goal may not be realistic, but you and your friends agree to get more information before deciding whether to pursue it.

3. You came up with an idea to develop an anti-bullying campaign in your school. When you shared this with a few friends, they wanted to join you in reaching this goal. Do you:
   a. discourage them from helping since you came up with the idea and want to do it on your own?
   b. let your friends help in ways that you decide, but you remain the main person working on this campaign?
   c. feel happy that you now have a committee working together to try to develop the campaign?

If you answered mostly 'a', then you are likely starting to learn about how to persevere, get organized, work with others, and pursue your goals.

If you answered mostly 'b', then you might be already working toward pursuing your goals but may benefit from the tips described in this chapter.

If you answered mostly 'c', then you seem to understand how to remain motivated, organized, and work toward your goals. Congratulations! Now you can read more about how to get started!

Breaking Down a Large Goal into Manageable Steps

Once you have decided on what you want to accomplish, it's time to focus on reaching your goal.

It can be hard to know where to start. Many people (kids and adults) may become overwhelmed when trying to think of the steps that they need to take to make a difference.

Do you already know how to break down a large goal into small steps? For example, is it easy or hard for you to break down a large school project into smaller steps?

Imagine that you have a class presentation to do, and you have a month to pick your topic, do your research, create a Powerpoint, and write a brief speech. Would you know how to budget your time and focus on each step to complete this task?

Think about what a ladder looks like. Maybe even draw one on a piece of paper. Now, put your goal at the top. When you get to the top of the ladder that means that you have reached your goal!

Think about the steps you need to take before getting there. On each step leading to the top, put a manageable activity or task that you can do within a few days or a few weeks to get closer to the top of the ladder or your goal.

Get it? It's less overwhelming when you think about achieving your goal one step at a time.

JEREMY'S STORY

Jeremy, a seventh grade student, thought it would be nice to send letters to all of the kids from his school district who were away at college for the first time.

Jeremy drew a ladder diagram and wrote his goal at the top of the ladder. He made a long ladder with many steps, so he could manage each step without too much pressure or anxiety. Here were the steps he created (from lowest to highest):

1. Ask Mom and Dad if they have any suggestions.
2. Discuss the idea with my principal and guidance counselor to see if it is feasible (e.g., can I actually get the students' addresses?).
3. If I get the addresses, then I need to print mailing labels for the envelopes. If the principal agrees to mail out the letters for me, skip steps 3, 5, and 6.
4. If my principal and guidance counselor say that my idea isn't possible, see if I can write a note to the first-year college students in the community newspaper instead.
5. Get envelopes and stamps to mail the letters. See if the school is willing to provide these.
6. Put the labels and stamps on the envelopes.
7. Speak to the class president and student council to see if they can get other kids in the grade to write letters too.
8. Write one letter, or more individual letters if warranted.
9. Edit the letter.
10. Print the letter.
11. Put the letters in envelopes and mail them out.

- Remember, this method could work for a lengthy school project or pursuing an altruistic goal.
- How would you have handled the situation if you shared Jeremy's dream?

> **If you get stuck and aren't sure how to break down a goal, don't be afraid to brainstorm with others.**

If you get stuck and aren't sure how to break down a goal, don't be afraid to brainstorm with others. For instance, if you want to stop teasing from happening in your school, it might be hard to figure out where to begin. Sometimes teachers have ideas and are just waiting for a motivated student to offer to help. The school psychologist or school social worker might even be familiar with research to point you in the right direction. So, speaking up and asking for help can be great skills to use as you are working toward your goals.

Decide on Your Plan

Now it's time to create your own ladder. Actually drawing a ladder and putting your goal at the top and the steps you need to take on the ladder's steps may help you to organize your plan and motivate you as you accomplish each task. This can be fun. Think about:

- your goal;
- the steps you need to take to reach it;
- how long it might take;
- what materials you need;
- whether you want or need adult support;
- whether you are going to complete the steps on your own or if it's better to work with others toward the goal.

It's not unusual to get stuck when you first try to reach a goal that seems important but very large. Perhaps your goal is to make the world more peaceful. Yikes! Where do you even begin? Remember, kindness can be contagious, so if you help create a more respectful atmosphere in your classroom, the people who are impacted by this may act kinder in other situations! And, if your strategy worked for one situation, you may want to try it again in a different situation. If you help decrease stress and increase empathy in your own everyday world, then you are already on the path toward making the world more peaceful.

Commit to Change

. . . .

It usually takes time and patience to achieve important changes. Imagine if Martin Luther King, Jr., Rosa Parks, Marie Curie, Mother Theresa, or Winston Churchill gave up their dreams after trying once or twice to have their message heard by the world. On rare occasions, change can occur quickly, but are you prepared to work over a longer period of time if that's what it takes to reach your goal?

Take some time (maybe this can be the first step in your ladder) to really think about your goal. Do you truly believe in it? Are you committed to work toward it, even if it takes a long time? If it doesn't seem practical right now, are you prepared to shape it into a more manageable goal?

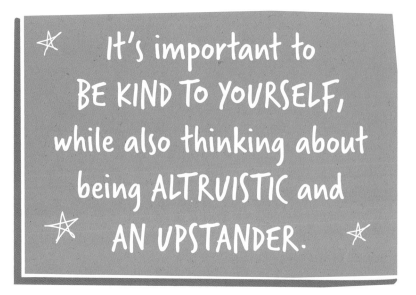

It's important to BE KIND TO YOURSELF, while also thinking about being ALTRUISTIC and AN UPSTANDER.

Working for a long-term—but important—goal can seem frustrating and exhausting. How can you stay motivated? Many kids have rewarded themselves (pat on the back; telling others about small accomplishments along the way; getting positive feedback) after completing a step toward the goal. Perhaps you can take time to do something fun for yourself. As you read earlier in this book, it's important to be kind to yourself while also thinking about being altruistic and an Upstander.

To Go Solo or Include Others

There is no "right" answer when it comes to reaching your goal on your own or working in a group. It depends on many things, including how you work best, whether there is so much to do that a group effort might speed things up, and whether working in a group would lead to collaboration and others sharing your dream.

If you have a great goal, but are shy, anxious, or you lack the confidence right now to speak up, this may be a good reason to ask friends or adults whom you trust to join your team. There is nothing wrong with inviting others to work toward a positive goal.

If you are outgoing and love being social, then you may enjoy working in a group more than working alone. Your motivation and ability to convince others to work together toward a common goal can be a goal on its own! If you show others—even just one or two others—that working toward a more peaceful world is a worthy goal, then you have already started the process.

Do you need all the credit for your goal and the plan to reach it? If so, you may resent others who work with you and then end up sharing the credit. If this is the case, you should consider your goal, and whether it's more important to be part of a team so you can pursue the goal more quickly or if it's more important to you to take sole credit.

> Your MOTIVATION and ability to convince others to WORK TOGETHER toward a common goal can be a goal on its own!

RACHEL'S STORY

Rachel, 9th grader, came up with a plan to pair her classmates with the 7th graders (youngest grade in her school building). She thought that the kids in the two grades could work on school improvement projects together. Rachel thought it would build community and social support at school.

Rachel began by asking her friends if they liked her idea. All of them commented that they loved the idea. They wanted to plan the program with her and present it to the guidance counselor. At first, Rachel felt angry. She felt like her friends were taking her idea away from her. Then she realized that she already accomplished the first step in her plan. She had motivated some of her classmates to participate in the program!

Rachel set up a meeting with her friends who were supportive of the program. She led the meeting, but then asked each member of the group for ideas on how to proceed. She delegated tasks, based upon what the kids volunteered to do.

Rachel and her group were successful in having one homeroom class of 9th graders paired with one homeroom class of 7th graders as a small-scale experiment to see how the plan worked. Rachel and her friends were happy that they were making a difference. They continued to pursue their goal of pairing the entire 9th grade class with the entire 7th grade class after the small-scale experiment was a huge success!

- How would you have felt if others wanted to join you in reaching a goal you created?
- Also, if you were Rachel, could you be pleased with not having the entire two grades connected but starting with a smaller experiment?

If you decide to work in a group toward a common goal, you may be able to accomplish the goal more quickly than if you did it alone. Here are some tips for doing this successfully:

- Brainstorm. Get everyone's opinion on how to reach the goal. You may find that someone knows a way to accomplish it more quickly!
- Ask everyone which step they are most comfortable doing.
- Break up into sub-groups (smaller groups), with each sub-group working on a different step at the same time, when possible.
- Schedule regular meetings to review what has been done, whether obstacles arose, and to decide what to do next.
- Show the others in the group that you appreciate them by listening to their opinions and genuinely complimenting their efforts. You may find that people are more willing to work hard to reach a goal when their efforts are recognized.

Sometimes, when people get together to work, they end up spending lots of time socializing without focusing on the goal. The ideal situation would be an atmosphere that's positive and social, where people continue to work together toward the goal.

Excluding Others

If you decide to work toward your goal in a group, do you think that you should allow everyone who is interested to join? You may feel that exclusion is mean or insulting, and that you don't want to reject anyone.

Including all who are interested is an idea that makes sense. It means that you have more people to help. But what if a bystander or even someone who has teased others wants to join your effort?

If it's clear that someone is joining your group only to make fun of your plans, then including this person will probably not be productive. Usually, though, kids who decide to spend time with others who are working toward a positive goal really want to be included.

You might use the opportunity to let these kids into your group and model positive interactions. It's helpful not to pre-judge a person who might really want to find a way to be more caring and kind.

Perseverance and Organization

There is a term called "Executive Functioning Skills" that is important for this discussion. Executive Functioning Skills are the skills people use to get started on projects, plan a timeline, gather materials, stay motivated, and so forth.

If someone is persevering, it means he can keep working, even if he is a long way from the ultimate goal. So, let's say that your goal is to encourage altruism from everyone in your community. You will have many steps to work on and may or may not fully reach this goal. Do you give up?

Can you keep working to achieve your goal, even if it will take a long time? If you are someone who gets discouraged easily and gives up, then set a goal you can reach quickly. Once this goal is hopefully reached, you can pick a new goal.

Even if you can work hard over time, are you also organized? Were you able to create the ladder with the steps needed to reach your goal? Did you get the materials you might need if you want to create posters? Did you set up a time to meet with other kids who want to join you? Being organized can save time because you won't find yourself suddenly looking for construction paper or texting friends to reschedule your meeting because you forgot to get materials or let the others know when you were hoping to meet.

Re-Evaluate Over Time

Sometimes people put a lot of energy into tasks and forget to think about whether they are actually getting closer to reaching their goal. If you have been working for a while and find yourself frustrated or that the goal now seems unrealistic, take a work break. It may be time to re-evaluate.

> If you have been working for a while and find yourself FRUSTRATED or that the goal now seems UNREALISTIC, take a work break. It may be time to RE-EVALUATE.

Here are some quick questions to ask yourself:

- Do I still want to reach the goal?
- Do I still think that the goal is realistic?
- What is frustrating me (if anything)?
- Do I need help from other students or adults?
- Should I change part of my strategy?
- Should I try to find a more immediate goal, but keep the larger goal in mind for the future?

Have you ever heard the phrase: "If at first I don't succeed, try, try, again" (originally written by T.H. Palmer)?

This is an important phrase to remind you to persevere or keep working. But, what if your goal is not realistic or your strategy isn't productive? At these times, it's okay to pause, breathe, review, re-evaluate, and then determine the right path to choose.

Abandoning an unrealistic goal and establishing an equally important and realistic goal is a sign of flexibility and adaptability!

Asking for Help

If you live alone on a deserted island, without internet service, it would be hard to ask for and receive help. Lucky for you, you probably live near lots of people.

Brainstorm with people and interview them for ideas. Ask for help if a step in your ladder requires adult assistance, and be proud that you are confident enough to ask for help when it's needed.

START SMALL!

Practice using the ladder method to organize your goals. Think about a project you need to work on or a test you need to study for. Now, break down your work or studying into steps on the ladder and put the goal at the top.

Think about whether you work well with others. If so, congratulate yourself! Having a group working toward a goal may speed up the process if everyone gets along and works well together. If not, but you think having a group working together would be useful, try using the skills of clear, respectful communication, compromising, and negotiation in an everyday situation, such as who goes first in a board game. These skills will likely come in handy when working with others later toward your goals.

8

BRAINSTORMING WAYS TO MAKE A DIFFERENCE

NOW THAT YOU HAVE THOUGHT ABOUT YOURSELF, YOUR skills, and your goals, it's time to move forward and start to make a difference. In this chapter, you will read about ideas—general and specific—that you can do at home, at school, in your neighborhood, and in the world.

Remember that you are reading suggestions. You don't have to do everything that is listed. If you take one of these suggestions, then that's great! Or, perhaps you have an idea that works better for you and for those around you.

It's wonderful if you see an issue, even if it's not in this chapter, and you decide to address it. Listing all the possible ways that a person can positively impact the world would take more than one chapter, more than one book—probably more than a few books. However, the possible goals described in this chapter may give you some general ideas of what you may want to start doing.

> Listing all the possible ways that a person can POSITIVELY impact the world would take more than one chapter.

Making a Difference in Your Home

Your home is a great place to practice being an Upstander and role-model. After all, it's probably where you spend a lot of time and where you may be able to make a big difference. Here are some ideas:

- Start with you! Can you use the relaxation skills and respectful communicating tools that you read about in Chapter 5 during disagreements with siblings or even adults in your home? This may not always be easy, but it's a way to model for others how to remain peaceful, even when upset.

- Try using positive self-talk rather than negative self-talk, so that you can remain confident and content before turning your attention toward helping others feel good about themselves.

- Spend time with others. Younger brothers and sisters often love to have the full attention of an older sibling. Why not spend time together, giving them the message that you value them and enjoy being with them? By doing this, they may be more confident and happier. Perhaps they will be more tolerant of others because of your actions.

- If you have an older sibling, try to find time when you can be together. Share in activities, laugh. Find out if your older brother or sister might want to work with you to make the world better. Maybe he or she even has ideas of what needs to be changed or what can be done.

- Compliment people in your home when they do something kind or when they overcome a challenge. Be specific on why you are giving the compliment.

- Consider writing a note to your parents about why you love them so much. Perhaps put it under or on their pillow (if you are allowed in their room), so they find that thoughtful surprise before going to sleep.
- Offer a helping hand to someone who needs it. For example, do a chore for someone or help your sibling study for a test if she agrees it would be helpful.
- If your siblings are in a conflict, offer to help them to work it out calmly and respectfully. You can even teach them about compromise and negotiation.

Making a Difference at School

While you are busy having fun with friends and focusing on your academic work, you may find yourself in situations where issues concern you. If you notice discrimination, bullying, or teasing, you can use the skills you learned in this book and decide if you should help directly or inform an adult (so they can assure the safety of those other students as well as keep you safe).

Here are some tips for how you can help at school:

- Try to include rather than exclude. It's fine to sometimes just want to be with your friends. But, at other times, you may feel that it would be helpful and even fun to include a student who seems to be alone or lonely.
- Work hard to avoid being a bystander who behaves negatively, even if it was never your intention (e.g., laughing because you were anxious). Try to

figure out a way to safely be an Upstander at those times.

- If a student has been out for a few days, why not send a quick text to see if he's okay? You would be letting him know that he matters!
- Compliment others—be specific and genuine.
- If a teacher or student is carrying a lot of books, why not offer to help if you aren't carrying too much yourself?
- Speak with other students to see what needs to be done to make your school more peaceful. Use your new skills to work in a group toward this goal.
- Is there a club for students who want to make a difference in the world? If not, can you talk with your guidance counselor or principal to see if they would agree to start one?
- Put up anti-bullying posters around the school, but get the permission of the principal or another staff member first.
- Would it be possible for you to help in a younger class periodically? You could pick some books about respect and problem-solving skills and read them to the students, if the teacher agrees.
- Use the Kindness Certificates that you read about in Chapter 4 to let others know that you recognize their kind actions.
- Include students from other groups when planning activities or projects. You might find that kids who don't usually socialize with each other have common interests!
- Remember reading about the power of a smile? Use that power and smile, and even say hello, to lots of different people so that they know that you are acknowledging them.

Making a Difference in Your Neighborhood

Whether your neighbors are people who live in your apartment building or people who live in houses on your street, think about how many of them you know. Do you know of ways that you can help them?

Before reaching out to others, think about whether they would want the help and whether your parents would approve.

If you want to help a person who is a stranger to you, it's important to talk with adults whom you trust first to make sure that it is appropriate and safe for you to reach out to that person. Unfortunately, there are times when a person may be unpredictable or not appropriate for you to be around.

Luckily, there are many altruistic acts that you can do in your community while keeping yourself safe at the same time. Think about the following:

- Do you know of neighbors who are physically unable to take care of some tasks? Could you help them? Perhaps you can take out their garbage once a week, offer to shovel snow, or walk their dog. If your neighbors want to pay you, try to let them know that you are doing this because it helps you to feel good. However, if they insist, think about buying something that they need with that money and giving it to them as a gift for a holiday or for their birthday, or donating that money to a charity.
- Is there a family friend or relative who your parents trust, you like, and who seems lonely? You might want to drop by periodically, just to say hello or to share a joke or a story. You don't have to spend a lot of time talking to become the highlight of that person's day!

119

- If you see that your neighborhood is littered with garbage, why not contact your local town hall to see if they can start a clean-up initiative. You should be very cautious about cleaning up litter on your own, though, since there's sometimes sharp glass or other items that can cause you harm.

- Do you and your friends want to work together to start a neighborhood campaign? First, think about what campaign you will pursue, then how you will pursue it. If you want to start a campaign that declares that your town supports kindness and peacefulness, why not make a few small sample posters to see if local stores and restaurants are willing to put them in their storefront windows?

- Do you think that kids need a place where they can hang out together after school? If your goal is to have such a place for lots of kids, brainstorm where they could meet. Is there a local YMCA, library, or even a religious establishment nearby? Why not contact them to see if they already have such a program and, if not, how you can help start one. You may need an adult, such as a parent, to help you get the attention of a staff member at one of these places, but don't be discouraged. The idea is yours, but why not get adults excited about your goal too?

- Some towns have geriatric or nursing facilities for the elderly and other people who can't live independently. At times, these places encourage kids and adults to come and keep the patients or residents company. Perhaps you could get the help of your music teacher to see if a group of you could go and sing at such a place. It could be fun for you and entertaining for those who live at the facility!

- You might be able to volunteer in the local library and read to the preschool kids. You could also ask if you can just help when they run preschool programs. Of course, only do this if you like young children.
- If an adult you know could contact someone at a local hospital and gain permission for you and your classmates to write get-well cards to their patients (general cards since you probably won't be getting the names of patients), then have fun knowing that each card has the potential to put a smile on the faces of people who are away from home and probably not feeling at their best.
- Use your power of words. If you are at a restaurant, take time to thank a helpful waiter. If a crossing guard helps you across a street, why not thank her? If you need help in a store, you can use "please" or "excuse me" to let the person know that you aren't taking him for granted.

Making a Difference in the World

Do you have a plan to impact people who you either don't know or who don't live near you? This can be complicated, but that does not mean it is impossible.

If you are motivated, try to think of a manageable and realistic goal that you can set and reach. Here are a few ideas:

- You may want to start helping people you know who don't live near you. For example, do you have a relative who lives far away from you? Why not periodically give him a call or send a card to let him know that you are thinking of him? Remember, if your relative feels appreciated and happy, he may spread this to others!

- Perhaps you want to help find a cure for a disease that has impacted someone you know. You may not know how to invent the cure, but you could raise money for research. Talk with your parents and, together, try to find a well-established organization that shares your goal. Are they working to raise money to fight the same disease? If so, you may want to contact them to see if they have proven ways that kids can help (e.g., sometimes they will send you materials so you can educate others and collect donations).

- If you want to contribute to a charity, think about ways to do this. Here are some tips:
  - Pick one of your birthday gifts to donate (if your charity supports homeless kids, for instance).
  - Start a lemonade stand and after you get the money, give it to an adult who can write a check. Then you can send a letter to the organization and include the check.
  - Register for a walk-a-thon organized by a charity and collect donations for each mile you walk.

- If you want to focus on stopping discrimination against groups of people, you could focus on inclusion at school. Then, you may want to contact some organizations that specifically have this same goal. Your teachers may be able to give you the name of an organization (e.g., Anti-Defamation League).

- If your goal is to create peace in the world, overall, you can also try to find people who share this goal. Look around your school and your neighborhood. You could also contact organizations, such as the Robert F. Kennedy Human Rights Center. Remember to always check with adults to make sure that any organization that you contact, including this one, is one that they feel comfortable having you communicating with directly.

Finding your goal can take time, but it can also be fun. Imagine yourself holding a magic wand that could instantly change something to make your home, school, neighborhood, or the world a better place. That's a good way to start.

Next, narrow down the goal so it is specific and you can reach it.

Then, remember to break down the goal into steps so you can watch your progress as you move, step by step, closer to your goal!

CONCLUSION

THIS BOOK HAS GIVEN YOU MANY TIPS TO HELP YOU ON your journey toward making a difference in the world. Now it's time to pair this knowledge with your inspiration and motivation to reach goals.

Here are a few things to remember as you work to become an Upstander:

- Be kind to yourself, not just to others.
- Expect some obstacles along the way. If you encounter a setback, consider whether your goals are unrealistic. If they are either unrealistic or will take a long time to reach, pause—then think about starting with a more immediate or realistic goal that you can attain more quickly or if you need to change your strategy.
- Learn to cope with stress so that you can model healthy coping strategies for others.
- Get help from an adult if the situation is serious or if there could be significant negative consequences if you speak up directly.
- Practice the skills of perspective-taking, empathy, and altruism.
- Kindness or anger can start a chain reaction.
- Sometimes it's more valuable to be able to compromise and negotiate than win a disagreement.

- If there's a rule you want to change, consider whether it's truly unfair or just not one that you like. Find out why the rule was put into place and think about the pros and cons of changing it.
- Set a goal that is realistic, specific, and attainable, and then break it down into smaller steps. This way, as you finish each step, you can know that you are on the path toward reaching your goal!
- Consider having others join you as you strive to make the world better. Working toward something positive could give those in your group a sense of pride. And working with others may help you to reach your goal faster than if you were working alone.
- Ask for help if you are unsure of how to proceed or if you encounter an obstacle.

This is the end of the book, but it may be the beginning of your great adventure. The world needs people who are motivated to make the world a more peaceful place. Congratulate yourself for being one of these people!

ABOUT THE AUTHOR

WENDY L. MOSS, PHD, ABPP, FAASP, HAS HER DOCTORATE in clinical psychology, is a licensed psychologist, and has a certification in school psychology. Dr. Moss has practiced in the field of psychology for over 30 years and has worked in hospital, residential, private practice, clinic, and school settings. She has the distinction of being recognized as a diplomate in school psychology by the American Board of Professional Psychology for her advanced level of competence in the field of school psychology. Dr. Moss has been appointed as a fellow in the American Academy of School Psychology. In addition, she is the author of *Bounce Back: How to Be a Resilient Kid, Being Me: A Kid's Guide to Boosting Confidence and Self-Esteem,* and *Children Don't Come With an Instruction Manual: A Teacher's Guide to Problems That Affect Learners;* coauthor, with Donald A. Moses, MD, of *The Tween Book: A Growing-Up Guide for the Changing You* and *Raising Independent, Self-Confident Kids: Nine Essential Skills to Teach Your Child or Teen;* coauthor, with Robin A. DeLuca-Acconi, LCSW, of *School Made Easier: A Kid's Guide to Study Strategies and Anxiety-Busting Tools;* coauthor, with Denise M. Campbell, M.S., of *The Survival Guide for Kids in Special Education (and Their Parents): Understanding What Special Ed Is & How It Can Help You;* coauthor, with Susan A. Taddonio, DPT, of *The Survival Guide for Kids With Physical Disabilities & Challenges;* and has written several articles. Dr. Moss has spoken on the radio about topics related to raising confident and independent children.

ABOUT MAGINATION PRESS

MAGINATION PRESS IS THE CHILDREN'S BOOK IMPRINT of the American Psychological Association. Through APA's publications, the association shares with the world mental health expertise and psychological knowledge. Magination Press books reach young readers and their parents and caregivers to make navigating life's challenges a little easier. It's the combined power of psychology and literature that makes a Magination Press book special.
Visit maginationpress.org.